ON

ROYCE

Griffin Trotter
Saint Louis University

Australia • Canada • Mexico • Singapore • Spain
United Kingdom • United States

Printed in the United States of America
1 2 3 4 5 6 7 04 03 02 01 00

For permission to use material from this text, contact us:
Web: http://www.thomsonrights.com
Fax: 1-800-730-2215
Phone: 1-800-730-2214

For more information, contact:
Wadsworth/Thomson Learning, Inc.
10 Davis Drive
Belmont, CA 94002-3098
USA
http://www.wadsworth.com

ISBN: 0-534-58388-1

Contents

Chapter 1 Absolute Idealism

Chapter 2 Loyalty

Chapter 3 God

Despite his gender, he attended his mother's School for Young Ladies and Misses. Here Josiah received nurture, training and guidance from a loving, omnipresent mother. Along with his sisters, Josiah came constantly under the spell of his mother's keen intellect, her stern sense of duty, and her evangelical spirit. Most certainly, the latter quality was amplified whenever father was around.

Near the age of eleven, Royce moved with his family to San Francisco, where his father peddled fruit (while proclaiming the gospel on street corners). That year, young Josiah was enrolled in Lincoln Grammar School. Here, as biographer John Clendenning notes, "the watchful protections of his mother and sisters gave way to the rude companionship of boys."[1] The awkward, shy and rather pudgy Royce learned that he was quite unsuited for the rough games that engaged most of his peers. And his intellectual superiority wasn't a great help either. He came across as a self-righteous blowhard, and he was teased mercilessly.

The sense of isolation and inadequacy that Royce experienced at Lincoln Grammar School profoundly affected his personality and his later efforts in philosophy. In an important way, his childhood struggle for personal identity continued throughout his life in his philosophy. It is likely that one of the first enduring victories in this struggle was the discovery of an intellectual niche. He learned early that he could stand his own in philosophical debate. Though Royce was inevitably the loser in playground fisticuffs, at Harvard he was characterized as "the John L. Sullivan of philosophy."[2] Still, his argumentative calisthenics were always tinged with a dash of humility. George Santayana wrote of Royce:

> If you gave him any cue, or even without one, he could discourse broadly on any subject... The tap once turned on, out flowed the stream of systematic disquisition, one hour, two hours, three hours of it, according to demand or opportunity. The voice, too, was merciless and harsh. You felt the overworked, standardised, academic engine, creaking and thumping on at the call of duty or of habit, with no thought of sparing itself or any one else. Yet a sprightlier soul behind the performing soul seemed to watch and laugh at the process. Sometimes a merry light would twinkle in the little eyes, and a bashful smile would creep over the uncompromising mouth. A sense of the paradox, the irony, the inconclusiveness of the whole argument would pierce to the surface, like a white-cap bursting here and there on the heavy swell of the sea.[3]

His zeal for argument, combined with persistently bungling social manners, ensured the permanence of Royce's social isolation (outside a close circle of family and friends). It is ironic that outcast Royce became America's greatest philosopher of community - but perhaps not surprising. Often it is those who experience the uncomfortable aspects of an object - its failures, pitfalls and tragedies - who are lured to study the object critically. Such was the case in Royce's study of community. Several other aspects of Royce's childhood also reemerge in his mature thought, and these provide a worthy preface to his philosophy. First is his sense that even the most dedicated individualists - people like the men who flocked to California's gold mines - are bearers of tradition. Young Royce was impressed by the manner in which frontier communities thrived on their laws, religious observances and customs - each inherited through generations of social life. This aspect of Royce's thought is expressed in his notion of the "community of memory," which we will discuss in Chapter 3.

Second is the importance of religion. Royce comments in the preface to his first major book that "religious problems have been chosen for the present study because they first drove the author to philosophy, and because they, of all human interests, deserve our best efforts and our utmost loyalty."[4] Related to Royce's emphasis on religious life is a third factor, his identification of the family as selfhood's central, formative crucible.

A fourth reemerging theme from Royce's childhood is his sense that uncritical acceptance of social or religious dogma thwarts human progress and begets suffering. In adulthood, Royce characterized himself as a nonconformist. Clearly this attitude began in California, where his reluctance to wholeheartedly embrace his father's beliefs caused friction. It is quite likely that Royce's need to think for himself and to critically address Christian dogma was a fundamental motive for his decision to pursue a career in philosophy.

In a similar vein, Royce believed that the interminable conflict and unrest characteristic of early California resulted from clashing expressions of unsophisticated and wrongheaded dogma. Early in his philosophical career, Royce expressed deep repugnance towards California and its provincialism. Later he grew wary about the "leveling effect" of a national mass media, and endorsed "wise provincialism" as an antidote to diffuse, uncritical social conformity.

Finally, Royce exhibited a lifelong preoccupation with the problems of suffering and moral degradation. Early in his wanderings along the California countryside, he came across a solitary miner's judgment. Perhaps the judgment refers to a kitten named Seattle. Or perhaps to an old Indian chief. Or does it refer to the seaport in the Pacific Northwest region of the United States? To answer these questions we need to know the intentions of the individual who formulated the judgment. If the intentions of this formulator are so vague that these questions cannot be answered, then the statement is meaningless – it is not a judgment at all. But if the formulator knows enough about the subject and predicate to specify the object of her judgment, then it would seem that she knows her object well and would not err. As Royce puts it:

> If I aim at a mark with my gun, I can fail to hit it, because choosing and hitting a mark are totally distinct acts. But, in judgment, choosing and knowing the object seem inseparable. [9]

The difficulty becomes more acute when we consider that there are apparently two Seattles in the aforementioned judgment. Imagine that Amy utters "Seattle is a city in Arkansas." The two Seattles in this case are (1) Amy's idea of Seattle and (2) the Seattle that is presumably an external object she hopes her idea accurately represents. But how can Amy know anything about a Seattle that is not part of her thought? Insofar as the external Seattle is indeed external, it cannot be part of Amy's thought and hence cannot be grasped or even intended in Amy's judgment.

Recall that Royce began the discussion of error by stating that the object of any judgment is something external to that judgment. Seattle's actual location, for instance, is external to Amy's judgment about Seattle's location. But now we find that the object of a judgment cannot be something external to thought. The object of a judgment, like the judgment itself, apparently must be an idea in the mind of the person who is making the judgment. Amy's judgment about Seattle's location is really only a judgment about one of her own ideas. If this is so, then error is even harder to explain. How can we be wrong about our own ideas?

Royce's answer to this question is the key to his philosophy, both in metaphysics and in ethics. Royce believes that our own intentions (or our "will" as he often calls them) are not entirely clear to us. We can be mistaken about what we mean and we can be mistaken about what we want. This insight will be developed much further in subsequent chapters, but in the context of Royce's argument from error the important point is that our knowledge of the intended objects of our judgments is incomplete. We know them well enough to pursue them, enough to identify their silhouette on the horizon of inquiry. But our knowledge remains unfulfilled just so long as we labor alone in the temporal world. Like the archer, we can miss the mark. In the case of our judgments, however, the mark is missed not because it is something external, but because we are unable to see it clearly.

Error is possible, then, because knowledge of our own intentions is incomplete. Still a problem remains if we leave the thinker within the isolation of her own thought. We have inferred that the objects of our judgments are our own ideas, and that each of us is fallible about specifying the nature of these ideas. But if such is the case, then the question arises: In what sense is it accurate to say that these ideas really have a definite nature? If our own ideas are not clear to us, how can they be clear at all? To whom are they clear?

One possible response would be to hold that the objects of any person's judgments are apt to become clearer over time. Hence, the truth or error of a judgment is something that occurs in that person's future experience. If Amy's idea of the city with a space needle and Ivar's Fish and Chips is so unclear that she thinks this city is in Arkansas, her error is apt to be revealed when she looks at a map, or perhaps when she hangs out with some folks from Seattle. In either case, Amy's idea of Seattle becomes clearer and more satisfactory through further experience. This response to Royce's problem is, in fact, the view held by Royce's friend William James. James called the theory that is partially expressed in this response the pragmatist theory of truth (though it diverges significantly from the theory of truth held by pragmatism's founder, Charles Sanders Peirce).

Several peculiarities pertain to this version of pragmatism. First, it is impossible on this view to say that a judgment is in error at the time the judgment is made. Error, like truth, happens to a judgment at some point in the future. Our ideas become erroneous when they fail to work out for us in experience. They become true when they work. Further, since our experience is never complete, even true judgments may later become false ones when they no longer work. What sense does it make, then, to say that the judgment was true or false at the time it was uttered or even at any determinate point along time's infinite progression? If the Jamesian response is correct, we must admit that the object of any judgment is an indeterminate future experience (or constellation of experiences) that does not exist at the time of the judgment. Royce writes:

Take the case of error about an expected future. What do we mean by a future time? How do we identify a particular time? Both of these problems plunge us into a sea of problems about the nature of time itself. When I say, *Thus and so will it be at such and such a future moment,* I postulate certain realities not now given to my consciousness. And singular realities they are. For they have now no existence at all. Yet I postulate that I can err about them. Thus their non-existence is a peculiar kind of non-existence, and requires me to make just such and such affirmations about it. If I fail to correspond to the true nature of this non-existent reality, I make an error; and it is postulated not merely that my present statement will in that case hereafter turn out false or become false, but also that it is now false, is at this moment an error, even though the reality with which it is to agree is centuries off in the future. [10]

This leads to other difficulties. Human beings are mortal. We tend to die before we complete our inquiries. Must we say that judgments are neither true nor false when their utterer dies before he is able to clearly specify his object? Further, since it always seems possible to be a little clearer about our ideas, shouldn't we defer all judgments until experience is complete, that is, until we have undertaken every possible investigation into the nature of our object? Obviously, such an investigation could never be complete. In what sense, then, is it accurate to say that error or truth happen to an idea? Finally, even if we experience some crowning event that brings perfect clarity to our judgments about a certain object, how can we determine with precision that this object is the same one that we intended at the instant of some prior judgment? Hence, James' theory fails to explain that most commonplace of human experiences, error. Our earlier questions remain unanswered. If our own ideas are not clear to us, how can they be clear at all? To whom are they clear?

Royce's response is that our ideas are perfectly clear and our intentions perfectly determinate, to an infinite consciousness that transcends the temporal restraints and cognitive limitations that impede human beings. This perfect knower is Royce's early philosophical version of God. Because the nature and qualifications of this God diverge somewhat from standard interpretations of the God of Christianity and other religious traditions, Royce initially avoids the term "God." Royce calls this perfect knower "the Absolute," reflecting the infinite scope of its consciousness and the finality and completeness of its ideas. We will investigate the theological characteristics of Royce's Absolute – i.e., the sense in which the Absolute is God – in Chapter 3. Our present concern, however, is to understand why Royce thinks that his Absolute provides the logical conditions for the possibility of error. To this end it is useful to examine a Roycean metaphor.

Suppose that two men, A and B, are permanently locked in separate closed rooms. Each has a "lantern contrivance" by which he can produce pictures on the wall of the other man's room. Neither man is aware of the pictures that he produces, nor even aware that he is producing pictures or that there is another room. Each is aware only of his own activities and of the pictures that are appearing on his wall. Now suppose A is a gifted inquirer and eventually hypothesizes that there is another room, much like his, and that the pictures on his wall result from the activity in the other room. Perhaps A learns to predict or even to manipulate the pictures in his own room by certain performances that produce changes in B's room, which in turn affect the pictures that B produces in A's room.

> In this case what difference does it make whether or no the pictures in A's room are actually like the things that could be seen in B's room? Will that make A's judgments either true or false? Even if A, acting by means that he himself cannot understand, is able to control the pictures on his wall by some alteration that he unconsciously produces in B's room and its pictures, still A cannot be said to have any knowledge of the real B and his room at all. And, for the same reason, A cannot make mistakes about the real room. He will, like a man in a dream, think and be able to think only of the pictures on his wall. And when he refers them to an outside cause, he does not mean by this cause the real B and his real room, for he has never dreamed of the real B, but only of the pictures and of his own interpretation of them. [11]

Royce holds that a major reason for our failure to immediately appreciate A's inability to err in these circumstances is the constant tendency to regard the matter from the point of view of a third person (which indeed is the viewpoint of the story's narrator) rather than from A's point of view. Minus a relationship to such a third person, A has no access to B.

> Now this relationship of A and B, as they were supposed to dwell in their perpetual imprisonment, is essentially like the relation that we previously postulated between two independent subjects. If I cannot have you in my thought at all, but only a picture produced by you, I am in respect to you like A confined to the pictures

produced from B's room. However much I may fancy that I am talking of you, I am really talking about my idea of you, which for me can have no relation whatever to the real you. [12]

Hence other thinkers, like external objects such as Seattle, are entirely beyond the grasp of thought. In the absence of contact with a master interpreter who is privy to our thoughts as well as to others' we have no means of appropriating their ideas as the objects of our own judgments. We do not really think about other persons or other objects. Hence, it is impossible for us to err about them. Instead, we think about our own thoughts and of these only reflexively, in the immediate moment (if such is possible), since time divorces us from our own prior and future thoughts. It seems that it is impossible to err just because each judgment can have nothing but itself as its object. If it intends as its object something else, then the idea is meaningless and hence not capable of being in error. If it intends itself, then the idea cannot be an error since it is, immediately, one and the same thing with itself. But now, once again, we are involved in the self-contradictory claim that error is impossible.

Royce holds that belief in the Absolute is necessary because the Absolute is the only way out of this contradiction. In other words, the Absolute provides the logical conditions that make error possible. Royce's Absolute is the interpreter, the omnipresent third person that allows finite thinkers to bridge the gap of time, as well as to establish a relationship between their ideas and the external world. For the Absolute, all eternity is comprehended in a single thought. A's hypothesis about B, as well as B's own thoughts, are comprehended and shared by the Absolute. A is capable of erring about B just because the Absolute clearly, completely and infallibly interprets A's judgments about B, specifying the objects of these judgments, and comparing these judgments directly, in one consciousness, with their objects. Further, the error in this case is really A's error, not an exclusive aspect of some separate realm of divine thought, because A is included in the Absolute.

Hence, Royce's God is no mere spectator, creating the world, then observing from on high. Royce's Absolute is the world. Everything that exists is an idea of God. Our own personal ideas – our thoughts and emotions – are God's ideas. Apparently non-sentient objects such as pencils, rocks and helium atoms are also God's ideas.

This may seem strange. Royce's view, in essence, is that the computer keyboard I press as I compose this sentence does not exist apart from the Absolute mind. It is an idea or thought, not an independent, material thing. Though this notion of external reality violates our common sense conviction that material things are independent of ideas, Royce has good reasons for holding it. These reasons may become clearer if we briefly examine the alternatives.

When we think about the things that exist, there are three basic approaches. Materialism is the doctrine that everything that exists is a material thing, and that mental things (like ideas and emotions) are merely expressions of the interactions between material things. The problem here is that materialists are hard-pressed to give an account of how purely physical entities could produce a mental phenomenon.

Another view, dualism, hypothesizes that there are two fundamental sorts of things – material things and mental things – that cannot be reduced to one another. The challenge for dualism is in explaining how mental things and physical things interact. How, for instance, does my will to move my arm (in the mental realm) result in an actual physical movement of my arm (in the material realm)?

A third view is idealism. As it was understood in Royce's day, idealism is the doctrine that the external world is a creation of mind. One obvious virtue of idealism is that it claims the existence of only one type of entity (mental) which is the only kind of entity we directly experience. Hence, it is not susceptible to the aforementioned challenges that confront materialism and dualism.

Modern idealism starts with Berkeley's theory that every external object is an idea, either of God's or of thinkers created by God (and sometimes of both). Sense perception, according to Berkeley, occurs when God causes our ideas. Further, the "objects" perceived by our senses are merely ideas in God's mind and would be wholly transitory if not for God's sustaining thought.

Kant developed a second form of idealism, called transcendental idealism. Transcendental idealism is the theory that ideas originate when the powers of the mind are counterposed on a wholly disorganized sense manifold. His theory derives its name from the fact that it is based on a transcendental argument – namely the argument that we must accept Kant's version of reality because it provides the only possible explanation (i.e., it provides transcendental conditions) for human knowledge. In Kant's theory, God drops out (except as a hopeful hypothesis), and there is no basis for upholding the sustained existence of external objects such as keyboards.

Finally there is absolute idealism, suggested in the works of Fichte and later developed more fully by Hegel, Bradley and Royce. According to this view, everything that is, is an idea conceived by an absolute consciousness. Hence, the subjective isolation of Kantian knowers (whose ideas are purely their own) is resolved in absolute idealism through the existence of a single, comprehensive thinker that takes everything existing throughout eternity as its immediate object.

Now the notion that my computer keyboard is an idea of the Absolute may be counterintuitive for two reasons. First, experience shows that the existence of the keyboard is sustained independently of my thought or of the thoughts of other finite thinkers. Second, since I have mental access to the keyboard (that is, I can perceive it) and I don't have access to the thoughts of other persons, I tend to think that the keyboard is a different kind of thing than thoughts are. Neither of these considerations prevents us from hypothesizing the existence of a higher form of thought, issuing from a more expansive consciousness, which shares our ideas, while also independently sustaining the keyboard. Royce and many other idealists would suggest that there is indeed, such a higher form of thought. There is nothing in experience that would preclude this hypothesis. And if Royce is right about the implications of his argument from error, then this version of idealism is the only viable way of interpreting reality.

For absolute idealism, our mental access to Absolute thought is guaranteed, since we are each part of the Absolute whole. That is, our thoughts are part of Absolute thought. My idea of the computer keyboard is identically the same idea as one of the Absolute ideas. The Roycean version of reality is that of an organic, infinite, conscious unity. Each human individual participates in this unity by comprising a particular aspect of the divine consciousness. Thinkers who conceive themselves apart from a relation to the Absolute are like a foolish man who loses his way in the woods. Suppose we ask the foolish man whether he has lost his way.

'I may have lost it,' he answers. 'But whither are you going?' 'That I cannot tell.' 'Have you no goal?' 'I may have, but I have no notion what it is.' 'What then do you mean by saying that you may have lost the way to this place that you are not seeking? For you seem to be seeking no place; how can you have lost the way hither?' [13]

This passage is vintage Royce. Born to a wandering, restless father; raised on stories of the apocalypse; ravaged by the contrast between mother's love and the cruelty of peers; Royce viewed life as a tumultuous journey. In the beginning, thought Royce, most of us are like the foolish man in the woods. Instinctively, we grope for personal fulfillment, indulging one, then another of our vague and shifting

12

desires. When satisfaction proves elusive, we become more critical. If we are smart and lucky, we manage to work out a plausible and consistent plan. However, unlike the mountain guide, with his destination firmly etched through many previous successful journeys, we must travel the wilderness in partial ignorance about our goal. We are explorers on a journey of discovery and our plan is tentative. Often it will need revision. Nevertheless, we can be certain that some final destination does really exist for us. There is knowledge to be discovered. Like the Pacific coast at the end of the Lewis and Clark expedition, our journey has a definite, if incompletely comprehended destination. This final destination (which includes the journey) for Royce is the Absolute. It is only through the Absolute that our judgments are finally vindicated or falsified, only through the Absolute that selfhood is fully achieved and morality fully understood.

But we are ahead of ourselves. Before examining the moral implications of Royce's absolute idealism, let us see how the doctrine stands up to critical scrutiny. In the following section we will enumerate several criticisms of Royce's absolute idealism. Then we will elucidate Royce's rejoinders.

Criticism of Royce's Absolute Idealism

Royce's initial version of the Absolute shares many similarities with Hegel's. In fact, Charles Peirce called Royce's first book on absolute idealism, *The Religious Aspect of Philosophy*, "an excellent introduction to Hegel." As we will see, the early Royce is vulnerable to many criticisms that had previously been directed at Hegel.

On the other hand, Royce always held that he was no more a Hegelian than he was a Kantian or a follower of several other important philosophers. He asked that if readers insisted on classifying him as a Hegelian, that they add a prefix – such as "Neo-," "Semi-," "Hemi-," "Pseudo-" or "Pleistocene-."[14]

In assessing the merit of Royce's absolute idealism and the extent of his Hegelianism, it helps to differentiate between Royce's argument for the existence of the Absolute and his theory about the nature of the Absolute. On the whole, Royce's argument (the Argument from Error summarized in the previous section) is rather more Kantian in form (as we shall explain below) than Hegelian, whereas his account of the Absolute was at first distinctly Hegelian. Criticisms of Royce's absolute idealism tended to be based either on (1) perceived logical deficiencies in his argument, or (2) concerns about the nature of his Absolute. Partially in response to this second brand of criticism, Royce's metaphysics became less and less Hegelian over time.

13

Criticism of Royce's Argument

Like Kant's arguments in the famous *Critiques*, the Argument from Error is a transcendental (not to be confused with "transcendent") argument. That is, it begins with some uncontested aspect of human experience (such as knowledge of the Pythagorean theorem, awareness of the intrinsic goodness of a good will or, in Royce's case, the possibility of human error) and then asks about the modes of cognition or reality (transcendental conditions) that must pertain in order to account for the experience.

Perhaps the central challenge for any transcendental argument resides in showing that certain conditions are not merely *sufficient* but also are *necessary* to explain the phenomenon in question. In a strict logical sense, transcendental conditions are not entailed by phenomena. Which is to say they do not follow from standard deductive arguments that begin by enumerating characteristics of these phenomena. Instead, transcendental arguments seek to discover conditions that are logically or cognitively prior to what they explain. This process often requires a difficult and comprehensive, yet unstructured conceptual analysis (such as exhibited in the Argument from Error). Since transcendental conditions cannot be deduced directly from the things they are conditions for, it always seems to remain an open question whether any proposed transcendental conditions are the only conditions that could pertain.

This sort of question was directed frequently at Royce's Argument from Error. As Shadworth Hodgson and others pointed out, even if Royce's Absolute is sufficient to account for error, it does not follow that it is the only possible explanation. For instance, we might observe, with James and the radical empiricists, that the connections between ideas in our stream of consciousness are as real as the ideas themselves. If James is right, there is a connection in consciousness between past and future ideas that potentiates knowledge of objects other than one's own current state of mind.

An analogy may be helpful here. Suppose I am a physician with an unconscious man as my patient. I notice the man has an odor of bitter almonds on his breath and I have ascertained that the man has not had access to almonds. Further, I go through every medically known cause of unconsciousness and find none that fit with this man's medical condition, except poisoning of the cytochrome oxidase system. I know that cyanide can poison the cytochrome oxidase system and that it can cause a breath odor of bitter almonds. Hence, I conclude that the man is suffering from cyanide poisoning. My reasoning process here is in some respects like Royce's transcendental argument. It begins with a phenomenon to be explained (the man's unconsciousness in one case, the possibility of error in the other) and arrives at the only explanation that is possible given the available information and modes of analysis. But have I proved my point? Medical knowledge – like the conceptual tools Royce applies in his argument – has no built-in guarantee of completeness. Perhaps there is something that isn't known or hasn't been covered. Or perhaps something crucial is simply beyond the grasp of human intellect. It is possible that my unconscious patient suffers from a rare, previously-unknown ailment of the cytochrome oxidase system. Likewise, it also seems possible that error could be explained by some ingenious new version of radical empiricism. In fact, Peirce claimed (with significant backing) that his own theory of continuous relations provided just that sort of explanation.[15]

Criticism of Royce's Absolute

The second common objection to Royce's absolute idealism is objection about the nature of his Absolute. Recall that the Absolute, on Royce's account, is an infinite, eternal consciousness that both creates and grasps all of reality in a single voluntary swoop. Since the Absolute is "all of reality" (nothing more, nothing less) this voluntary swoop is an act of self-creation. That is, the Absolute is all that exists and it is the cause of all that exits. Every fact is a fact wholly because it is an object of God's will, that is, a fulfillment of God's purpose. And every fact is related to every other fact because each fact is ultimately comprehensible only through the unity of the divine Will.

Two aspects of this characterization of Absolute reality should be noted from the outset. First, it is monistic. Ultimately, the universe is a single comprehensive unity, a single thought of the Absolute. Second, it is voluntaristic. That is, reality is an act of will. It is a self-fulfilling purpose, unconstrained by any external principle, creating its own laws and standards of morality.

Since most of Royce's commentators were also voluntarists (of one stripe or another), criticism tended to be directed towards his monism. George Holmes Howison claimed that Royce's theory was pantheistic.[16] Pantheism is the doctrine that God is all-inclusive and hence that God is not separate from man or from nature. Howison's concern was that Royce's monism allowed no space for personal (as opposed to divine) purposes, foibles and destinies. Howison's critique had some sting as an expression of traditional Western theism (which excludes pantheism).

Peirce observed that Royce's Absolute is not really God in any practical sense. It is not a warm, inviting parental type, nor is it an easily comprehensible source of guidance. He held that the Absolute was, pragmatically speaking, too abstract to be of use to ordinary Huckleberry Finn sorts who practice Christianity without the support of metaphysical theories.[17]

In a similar vein, James complained that the only practical implication of Royce's Absolute is that it allows everyone to take a "moral holiday." Since the Absolute provides an advance guarantee of perfect outcomes, people can relax and set aside their schemes for improving the world. On James' account, Royce's theory is deterministic. That is, it leaves no room for human freedom or human agency. It is a voluntarism, yes, but the entire prerogative seems to be with God, not humanity.[18]

These criticisms cut to the heart of Royce's project. Recall the three elements Royce ascribed to any religion: (1) moral instruction, (2) inspiration and (3) a theory about the nature of things that supports the first two elements. Peirce held that Royce's absolute idealism fails on all three counts because it is too abstract. James claimed, in essence, that Royce's absolute idealism fails to provide moral instruction or inspiration because it fails to provide an arena for human agency.

Royce's Response

Royce spent the better part of twenty-five years (from 1885 until 1910) defending the conception of the Absolute developed in *The Religious Aspect of Philosophy*. This period corresponds roughly with Royce's "middle period," since it was transitional between his earlier radical empiricism (strongly influenced by William James, but not covered in this volume) and his later interpretive theory of reality (strongly influenced by Charles Peirce).[19] Much of his work during this middle period consisted of working out the practical implications of his theory. Royce sought to provide flesh and blood to the bare-bones system he had abstractly worked out through the argument from error.

First Response: Internal and External Meaning

Royce's response to criticisms about the logic of his argument from error was indirect. He sought to clarify the argument rather than to provide a substantial defense of its structure. This response makes sense insofar as the logical import of transcendental arguments resides in the clarity with which transcendental conditions are linked (non-deductively) to the phenomena they explain. As Descartes observed in his *Meditations*, the validity of some arguments can be assessed only from the vantagepoint of a thinker who clearly apprehends all its premises in a single act of cognition. Insofar as Descartes' assessment applies to the argument from error, a process of clarification is the best way to investigate it.

Royce's doctrines of voluntarism and monism entail that everything that is, is the fulfillment of a purpose, and that all our individual purposes are ultimately expressions of a single purpose – the Absolute purpose, which seeks itself. To clarify this relation, Royce distinguished provisionally between the internal and external meaning of ideas.

The internal meaning of an idea is its conscious purpose.[20] It is internal in the sense that it is what someone privately has in mind when she formulates the idea; it is her plan of action or thought. The external meaning of an idea, on the other hand, is the fulfillment of this purpose; it is a feature of reality that is in some way external (through separation in time or space) to the idea that seeks it. It is the object of an idea.

Judgments, like all ideas, are purposive. People who make judgments aim, if they are sincere, to express a fact or truth. That is their internal meaning, or at least part of it. If they aim at something else, their thoughts are not really judgments (though they are clearly purposive). In order to express a fact or truth, judgments must succeed in at least two ways. They must seek out an intended object and they must be related to this object in the intended way. That is, their internal meaning must be fulfilled. They must have an external meaning.

Against the charge that Royce's Absolute is only one of several conceivable ways of explaining the possibility of error, Royce responds that it is inconceivable that external meaning, which is the fulfillment of a purpose, could be explained apart from internal meaning, which is the purpose that it fulfills.

Hence, the idea and its object are linked in a way that crude metaphysical realism (which holds that external objects of knowledge are wholly independent of ideas) cannot explain. Since the linkage between internal and external meanings cannot be established in finite thought (due to previously discussed cognitive and temporal barriers), reality must include infinite thought. Further, an infinite variety of ideas and objects can be integrated within the scope of a single, infinite purpose.

Because Absolute thought is self-fulfilling, internal meaning and external meaning are ultimately equivalent. The Absolute is the object of its own thought. Error is possible, however, from the standpoint of finite thinkers because internal meanings are often obscure. We do not always comprehend our own purposes. To clarify this segment of his argument, Royce invokes another distinction.

Second Response: Wide and Narrow Aspects of Will

Royce employs two senses of "will." In a wide or deep sense, will is the entire purposive side of consciousness, including indeterminate purposes of which we are only vaguely aware. In a narrow or shallow sense, will consists only of purposes that we are able to recognize at the moment.

For example, suppose third-grader Roger wills to ace his spelling test. From his point of view, his purpose in this endeavor is to learn the correct spelling of certain words so that he earns a good grade and receives praise from his parents. These purposes comprise the narrow aspect of his will. However, he also wills to establish a sense of unique personal identity and worthiness, and to integrate his actions into a fulfilling life plan. These latter aims are not yet explicit for Roger. They are part of his will in the wide sense.

Royce believes that the ultimate purpose of thought (and action) is to bring our will into full consciousness. We strive to reconcile the narrow will with the wide one. This goal is achieved by making vague internal meanings more determinate. Error is possible because the things that we will (in the narrow sense) may obscure rather than illuminate our deepest internal meaning. In *The World and the Individual*, Royce writes:

> And what this way of stating our problem implies may first be illustrated by any case where, in doing what we often call 'making up our minds,' we pass from a vague to a definite state of will and of resolution. In such cases we begin with perhaps a very indefinite sort of restlessness, which arouses the question, 'what is it that I want? What do I desire? What is my real purpose?' To answer this question may take a long time and much care; and may involve many errors by the way, errors, namely in understanding our own purpose. Such search for one's own will often occupies in the practical life of youth, some very anxious years. Idleness, defective modes of conduct, self-defeating struggles without number, fickle loves that soon die out, may long accompany what the youth himself all the while regards as the search for his own will, for the very soul of his own inner and conscious purposes. In such cases one may surely err as to one's intent. The false or fickle love is a sort of transient dream of the coming true love itself. The transient choice is a shadow of the

coming true choice. But how does one's own real intent, the object at such times of one's search, stand related to one's present and ill-defined vague restlessness, or imperfectly conscious longing. (sic) I answer, one's true will, one's genuine purpose, one's object here sought for, can be nothing whatever but one's present imperfect conscious will in some more determinate form. What one has, at such times, is the will of the passing moment, – an internal meaning, consciously present as far as it goes. But what other, what external meaning, what fact beyond, yes, what object, is the goal of this quest? I answer, nothing whatever in heaven or in earth but this present imperfect internal meaning rendered more determinate, less ambiguous in its form, less a general longing, more a precisely united and determinate life.[21]

In this marvelous passage, Royce goes beyond mere clarification of his previous argument from error. He begins to articulate his response to critics (such as Peirce and James) who suggested that his theory was mere abstraction, devoid of major practical implications. Royce argues that his theory of the Absolute provides a foundation for the articulation of personal aims. Writing long before Sartre or Erickson, Royce suggests the presence of an identity crisis, often peaking in youth, but played out over the scope of one's entire life. This crisis, explains Royce, emerges from the discrepancy between one's current vague sense of individual purpose and the comprehensive purpose that flows from the Absolute. The latter is our own, true purpose – an aspect of the Absolute purpose that provides, for each individual, the basis for a unique life plan. But how is such individual fulfillment consistent with the singularity of the Absolute? How can Royce's monism be reconciled with the pluralism implied by his notion of unique life plans? To answer these questions, we need to examine Royce's account of individuality.

Third Response: The Criterion of Individuality

Our ideas can err, Royce argues, just insofar as they may be classified as our own ideas, somehow separate from the totality of knowledge that completes them. And this partial separation of ideas is possible just insofar as our lives and our ideas maintain the stamp of individuality. That is, error is possible because our vague and imperfect personal striving has permanent significance; because it is recognized by the Absolute as a legitimate aspect of the divine purpose. Hence, my failures are important failures, even if they are ultimately overcome through the unifying activity of the Absolute.

19

two athletes, performing in unison? Royce uses these and other human experiences as philosophical building blocks.

Interestingly, one of the fathers of contemporary analytic philosophy aptly expresses why Royce, in contrast to most current members of the analytic school, is so uniquely relevant for the contemporary intellectual. Bertrand Russell approved of Royce because he was attentive to "whispers from another world." As Russell notes: "The greatest men who have been philosophers have felt the need both of science and mysticism: the attempt to harmonize the two was what made their life, and what always must, for all its arduous uncertainty, make philosophy, to some minds, a greater thing than either science or religion."[22] Despite endless proclamations of secular humanism, the world is filled with individuals who attend, with Royce, to these mysterious whispers.

Many of Royce's contemporaries thought of his philosophy as Hegel's last gasp, and this attitude is shared by some contemporary philosophers. However, to equate Royce's thought with Hegel's, just because both were absolute idealists, is comparable to equating the political thought of Abraham Lincoln with that of Richard Nixon, just because both were Republicans.

In distinction to Hegel, Royce believed that adequate knowledge is, from the standpoint of current inquirers, infinitely remote.[23] Hence, Royce (like Peirce) is committed to a pluralism of ideas and communities – thus maximizing our sources of viable hypotheses – whereas Hegel urges more comprehensive social organization. Royce also repudiates Hegel's logic, replacing Hegelian dialectic with a less confrontational, more mathematical, triadic version of inquiry. For Royce, pluralism is a healthy way of pursuing various common ideals mutually held by otherwise diverging communities of inquiry.

Perhaps the distinction between Royce and Hegel is best expressed in Royce's comments about the latter:

> Hegel, as we see, makes his Absolute, the Lord, most decidedly a man of war. Consciousness is paradoxical, restless, struggling. Weak souls get weary of the fight, and give up trying to get wisdom, skill, virtue, because all these are won only in the presence of the enemy. But the absolute self is simply the absolutely strong spirit who bears the contradictions of life, and wins the eternal victory.[24]

Though Royce agrees that human fulfillment can be achieved only through strenuous effort, suffering and travail, he does not subscribe wholeheartedly to the metaphor of battle, nor does he recapitulate Hegel's tendency to isolate enemies. Royce's comments on Hegel tend to portray the German idealist as an intellectual bully, more concerned with establishing his own position in the academic hierarchy than with expressing the humility and sensitivity of sublime religion. Royce's Absolute, in distinction to Hegel's, is as much comforter as warrior, providing solace rather than merely challenging us to enter the fray.

Throughout his career, Royce gradually modified and reinterpreted his notion of God. In the long run, his position is much closer to that of fellow American Charles Sanders Peirce than to Hegel's. However, before examining Royce's religious philosophy or his Peircean turn, it is instructive to look at his ethical philosophy, i.e., his philosophy of loyalty.

Endnotes

1. John Clendenning, *The Life and Thought of Josiah Royce*, revised edition (Nashville: Vanderbilt University Press, 1999), 32.
2. John Jay Chapman, "Portrait of Josiah Royce, the Philosopher," *Outlook* 120 (2 July 1919): 372-77. John L. Sullivan was the premier boxer of Royce's day.
3. George Santayana, "Josiah Royce," in *Character and Opinion in the United States* (New Brunswick: Transaction Publishers, 1991), 97-138.
4. Josiah Royce, *The Religious Aspect of Philosophy* (Boston: Houghton, Mifflin and Company, 1885), v. Hereafter, this book will be abbreviated RAP.
5. Joseph McCarthy was an American politician who took the lead in searching out and prosecuting communists during the "Red Scare" of the 1950s. The lives of many innocent people were ruined.
6. RAP, 6. This chapter of RAP ("Introduction") is reprinted in John K. Roth, ed., *The Philosophy of Josiah Royce* (Indianapolis: Hackett Publishing Company, 1982), 35-43. Hereafter, *The Philosophy of Josiah Royce* will be abbreviated PJR.
7. RAP, 3-4. PJR, 37.
8. RAP, 397. PJR, 52.
9. RAP, 399. PJR, 54.
10. RAP, 418. PJR, 65.
11. RAP, 414. PJR, 63.
12. RAP, 416. PJR, 64.

naturally present within myself. By nature I simply go on crying out in a sort of chaotic self-will, according as the momentary play of desire determines.[3]

Royce defines the self as "a human life lived according to a plan" and holds that to have a plan is to have an ideal. The cultivation of this personal ideal he calls "idealization." The paradox of individuation results because idealization – which aims at establishing unique individuality – can be achieved only with a degree of conformity. In what respect is a personal ideal really personal if it is acquired from parents, peers or other socio-cultural influences? How can we forge a unique and fulfilling personal identity when the tension between individualism and social conformity is apparently irresolvable? These are questions that lurk in the depths of every adolescent or mid-life identity crisis. They express a central – perhaps even *the* central – problem of twentieth century humanity. Since this problem is not unique to our age, Royce's first step in addressing it is to see how ordinary people have responded over the years. In this Roycean spirit, let us temporarily dispense with metaphysical abstractions and examine some of the ideals that have inspired persons – young and old – to navigate their own life plans.

Three Moral Ideals

Idealization generally begins in the home, where a broad (and sometimes strange) array of idols, fairy tails and metaphors tend to circulate. Consider my own household as an example. Everyone in my family is an animal. My wife is an eagle because her fine arts background allows her to soar majestically above the rat race. One son is a tiger, because he's cagey, athletic and smooth. Another son was born to run, sprinting everywhere he goes – even to bed. He's a mustang. I'm a wolf because I hail from the mountains and admire loyalty above all virtues. Finally, there is Shane: the bear. Shane is a big boned, red haired, freckle faced 11-year-old who always wears a smile. He can press about 100 pounds (making him by far the strongest kid in school), but meanders about so casually and grins so readily that none of his classmates ever perceive him as a threat. His favorite thing in the world is a back rub. Last month, I saw him scratching against a tree trunk, munching on some berries. Sometimes I think he really is a bear.

I first came up with the idea of assigning each kid a representative animal when I was at a toy store in Zurich, shopping for gifts to bring home after a long excursion. Eventually, I bought a stuffed animal for each family member, and wrote short essays describing the virtues of the animals and how they fit with the personalities of my wife and kids. I could have never guessed the profound effect these gifts would have on my children and on the family dynamics.

The kids were thrilled by what they perceived as a concrete embodiment of their own nobility, uniqueness and self worth. Almost immediately, they perceived themselves and their actions through the symbolism of their animal identities. Shane's walls are now plastered with Chicago Bears memorabilia, and, as we would expect from the human embodiment of a grizzly bear, he intends to play linebacker professionally (after a 4-year stint with the Montana Grizzlies). When he resists bedtime, I remind him that bears are strong because they hibernate, and the matter is settled. Once, he became lackadaisical during a soccer game. Unaware of the fury I was about to unleash, I called him to the sideline and told him that bears are very ferocious when things get tough. Before I could blink, he was running over an opposing player and pounding the ball into the net. In the next five minutes, Shane transformed the soccer field into his personal hunting grounds, scoring two goals and drawing a roughness penalty. After the game, his coach exulted, "Shane you were like a man possessed." I corrected him. "Not a man, coach, a bear."

All good parents strive to help their children establish meaningful goals and to develop the self-esteem that is necessary to pursue them effectively. Before they became bears and tigers and mustangs, the Trotter kids heard a thousand times about the importance of honesty, scholarly achievement and other worthwhile ends. They were subjected to concise accounts of the moral virtues and praised effusively when they exhibited them. Yet, like most parents, my wife and I had a sense that the more elusive and abstract values were difficult to describe, and even more difficult to sell. Even when the kids temporarily grasped the meaning of courage, or loyalty, or love, it wasn't clear that they really cared. This difficulty eased when the messages were presented through the animal metaphors. Now our sons have something they can sink their teeth into. They are inspired.

Animal metaphors illustrate the power of personality ideals in moral instruction. They are useful even for adults. I know a successful businessman who considers himself a rhinoceros (because he is a hard charger) and begins each day with a rhinoceros chant, bellowed out while he is showering. Nevertheless, we will not solve the paradox of individuation by patterning ourselves after animals. Animal metaphors are useful for supplementing a personal ideal, but they are not comprehensive ideals. For one, there are not enough species to assure each human being a unique identity. More importantly, human beings are quite different than our animal friends. We have different concerns and different habits than bears and tigers do. We are also more intelligent and more adaptable. Royce preceded John Dewey in identifying plasticity (the capacity for intelligent adaptation to the environment) as the most characteristic feature of the human species. Any adequate moral ideal will highlight this feature.

As a preface to our account of Royce's favored personality ideal, let us see how Royce evaluates three historically prominent (but not quite sufficient) moral ideals.

The Hero

The hero is one of the oldest and perhaps the most prominent general moral ideal. For Royce, the hero is

> a person who, in a given social order, is admirable or ideal by virtue of his great powers, of his great services to his community, and of the admirable and distinguished deeds by which he wins a kind of literal and worldly prominence. [4]

Royce found much of value in the heroic ideal. Any satisfactory moral ideal must be inspiring, and stories of heroes can be outstanding in this regard. Heroes express cultural values and are responsive to community needs. The athletic hero is required to cooperate with teammates for a common goal. Patriots and political heroes are defined by their service. Even heroic artists, inventors and others who pursue rather solitary passions are valued primarily for their social contributions.

The legacy of heroes precedes civilization. Heroes are evident in tribal myths and ancient oral traditions. Certain cultures, such as Homeric Greece, center on heroism. Celtic hero Cù Chulaind illustrates the typical orientation of such cultures:

> 'A good day, then,' said Cathub, "for who takes arms today will be great and famous – and short-lived.' 'Wonderful news that,' answered Cù Chulaind, 'for, if I am famous, I will be happy even to live just one day.'

Cù Chulaind here expresses one of heroism's crucial aspects. To be a hero one must be socially recognized. The hero is an exemplar of human excellence in a valued realm of human activity. But mere virtuosity is not enough. The virtuoso must be appreciated.

Examples of failed heroism abound. Josh Gibson, who played in the old Negro leagues, was perhaps the greatest baseball player who ever lived. However, his exploits were not widely recognized or publicized. Hence he was not a hero in the classical sense investigated by Royce. Jackie Robinson, on the other hand, was inferior to Gibson as a baseball player but became a hero due to the massive publicity and (eventually) appreciation he received.

The discrepancy between Gibson and Robinson directs us to the major difficulty with heroism as a moral ideal. Heroism depends on factors that are well beyond the control of the aspiring hero. It requires good fortune. And it requires talent. Moral ideals are useful because they provide an image of we ought to strive for. Luck and talent, however, are not acquired through effort. Heroism becomes, for the average child, an impossible and frustrating ideal. Most of us will not become Michael Jordan or Abraham Lincoln.

The Self-denying Self

Royce called the second moral ideal the "self-denying self." This once-popular ideal is illustrated in the lives of various saints, mystics and martyrs. Arthur Schopenhauer championed the self-denying self, and thought it was the highest ethical ideal. Sören Kierkegaard and Friedrich Nietzsche also described versions of this ideal, but found them deficient.

Self-denying selfhood begins with awareness that human beings are irreparably flawed:

> From this second point of view what I am is always so incomplete that it is rational to observe that by nature I am whatever I ought not to be. For if I were what I ought to be, my acts would conform to a single purpose. But by nature I neither know any single purpose of life, nor conform my acts even to such purposes as now seem to me to be the highest. The way of life, therefore, depends upon first learning a thoroughgoing self-denial.[5]

In essence, the self-denying self is an individual who wills not to have a unique will. As Nietzsche observes, there is an effort to extinguish personal will through an act of personal will. This rather paradoxical objective is achieved by cultivating an attitude of detachment.

Royce was exposed to the self-denying self at a very early age. In many ways, his mother embodied this ideal. A characteristic strength of the self-denying self is calmness in the face of worries, frustrations and

31

tragedies. Unsurprisingly, Royce finds this ideal attractive.

The basic insight of the self-denying self – that human beings are inevitably flawed – is part of the problem of evil that Royce addresses with such restless persistence. Royce also agrees with the self-denying self in holding that moral virtue requires discipline. If we are to hear whispers from our deepest will or internal meaning, we must quiet the storm of transitory emotions.

Ultimately, however, Royce agreed with Nietzsche's opinion that the asceticism of the self-denying self is based on a mistake. According to Nietzsche, self-denial is really an expression of self-affirmation, deprived of the zest for struggle. The Nietzschean Titan, Zarathustra expresses this criticism:

> Even in your folly and contempt, you despisers of the body, you serve yourself. I say to you: your self itself wants to die and turns away from life. It is no longer capable of what it would do above all else: to create beyond itself. That is what it would do above all else, that is its fervent wish.[6]

Though Royce and Nietzsche interpreted and carried out the desire for creation beyond the temporal self in radically different ways, it is interesting to note that both thinkers feel this desire deeply. In the end, they reject the self-denying self because of a belief in the creative office of humanity.

In broad terms, the ideal of the self-denying self falls prey to the criticism that Howison levied against Royce's initial formulation of absolute idealism. It provides no concept of individuality. Though Royce wanted to preserve his Absolute, and the notion that we are aspects of the Absolute life, he was also keen to establish the uniqueness and intelligence of persons. Instead of being a unique and exemplary part of the whole, the self-denying self is content to be merely a part of the whole. Royce could not accept this limitation.

Contemporary sociologist Eric Hoffer has documented serious dangers that pertain when communities cultivate self-denying selves.[7] Hoffer's image of the "true believer," one who unthinkingly manifests the will of a higher social power, is perhaps the most comprehensive portrait of the self-denying self in current scholarship. According to Hoffer, when people deny or eradicate their own selfhood, they are prone to becoming thoughtless pawns and fanatics in the service of some overly simplified social formulation or of a charismatic leader. Unfortunately, his thesis has been illustrated in tragedies at Jonestown, Bosnia and elsewhere. Royce's critique of "mob spirit" precedes

Hoffer's inquiry, and voices many of the same concerns.

The Rebel

The third moral ideal is radical self-assertion, an image that Royce attributes to Nietzsche. Its exemplar is the titan or the rebel. Royce also calls it the defiant personality.

Rebellion is an accurate moniker, for this ideal consists largely of negative reaction to the prior ideals. According to the rebel, aspiring heroes are hopelessly naïve, somehow failing to observe nature's inherent whimsy and failing to perceive that they are slaves to the dominant ideology. Those who aspire to self-denial, on the other hand, are hypocrites because (as Nietzsche observes) their self-denial is essentially a contorted form of self-assertion.

The rebel defies the conventionality of the hero and the hypocrisy of the self-denying self by affirming his or her otherness. This defiance is of value for Royce insofar as it expresses "one of the deepest insights of humanity, namely the insight that the self must always in the end be its own ethical director, and that the ideal cannot be defined merely in terms of fortune."

This insight is, of course, the message we recognized earlier in Royce's principle of autonomy. It is what led us to the paradox of self-realization. If we discard every social influence in the name of personal authenticity, there is nothing left to constitute this authentic person we so vigorously wish to become. An appeal to other persons is inevitable, as Royce observes:

> The ideal of a Titanic self-assertion hardly ever utters itself without showing that the whole value of this self-assertion can become real only in case there is a genuine life, having a social meaning, and a life in which the ideal gets a concrete expression.[8]

Because the rebel is so wary of overt conformity, she most frequently expresses the social impulse in terms of objections against some evil (often conformity itself). There are two ways in which such objections achieve the necessary social connections: First, rebellion may be a collective effort. Often the rebel enjoys the fellowship, guidance and approval of fellow rebels. Solidarity among rebels may be extraordinary. And of course solidarity requires a degree of conformity. It is no mistake that adolescents persecute peers who fail to express the same "non-conformist" styles, tastes and mannerisms that define their rebellion. Vulnerable youths are typically uncomfortable with rebellion unless all their friends are doing it too.

A second way in which rebellion establishes social ties is by eliciting a response from targeted individuals. Even negative feedback is valuable. It becomes a form of self-verification for those who define themselves as opponents of someone else. This aspect of rebellion is quite paradoxical. Rebellion as a criterion of identity requires the persistence of whatever evil it ostensibly seeks to eradicate. If personal identity is primarily understood as rebellion against a particular evil, then the individual becomes less of a person – or not a person at all – when the evil is dispatched.

Both of the aforementioned sources of sociality are problematic. In the first, rebellion contradicts itself by requiring conformity. Hence the paradox of self-realization is exacerbated. In the second, rebellion breeds hostility, resentment and an imperative for ever more elaborate proofs that the enemy is still present. Such divisiveness and contrivance are hardly the characteristics we seek in a moral ideal.

The difficulties with a morality of rebellion extend far beyond the scope of adolescence. In history, they are manifest whenever revolutions are precipitated primarily by resentment rather than by commitment to a viable positive ideal. The bloody aftermath of the French Revolution exemplifies the dire consequences of rebellion that is not augmented by forward vision.

Hence Royce is not satisfied with rebellion as a comprehensive moral ideal. This is not to say he disapproves of rebellion. Often it is necessary. Some of the greatest moral achievements of our age have resulted from just rebellions waged by feminists, civil libertarians and others. But there must be something else as well. What will happen to the feminist when she wins her victory against gender discrimination? Will academic departments of feminist studies disband and their professors look for another vocation? Or will feminists become sophists, employing a highly specialized hermeneutic of suspicion that discovers the oppression of women in every situation? If rebellion is understood as a comprehensive moral ideal, the latter option may be the only alternative to the collapse of feminist culture.

Loyalty

Royce finds his solution to the paradox of self-realization, and synthesizes salient elements of heroism, self-denial and rebellion, through the ideal of loyalty.

Loyalty Defined

Royce's preliminary definition of loyalty, offered in the first chapter of *The Philosophy of Loyalty*, is "the willing and practical and thoroughgoing devotion of a person to a cause." Let us examine the elements of this definition.

First and foremost, loyalty requires a cause. According to Royce, a cause is something that loyal individuals value intensely and pursue socially. It derives its value from sources beyond the solitary individual and it is more than a summation of various individual wants or needs. Royce writes:

> The cause to which a loyal man is devoted is never something wholly impersonal. It concerns other men. Loyalty is social. If one is a loyal servant of a cause, one has at least possible fellow servants. On the other hand, since a cause, in general, tends to unite the many fellow-servants in one service, it consequently seems to the loyal man to have a sort of impersonal or superpersonal quality about it. You can love an individual. But you can be loyal only to a tie that binds you and others into the same sort of unity, and loyal to others only through the tie.[9]

A cause, then, is a tie that binds. It is not possible in Roycean terms to be loyal to an individual. Rather loyalty is directed to a value that individuals share. In this sense, Royce's concept of loyalty is similar to Aristotle's version of friendship. According to Aristotle, the highest form of friendship is based on shared notions about what is morally good. Affection is directed not merely at the friend, but at the moral ideal that supports the friendship.

In fact Royce holds that a friendship is a sort of community, defined by the values shared therein. These values are the cause that animates loyal friends. When Royce says that loyalty is devotion to a cause, he means that it is devotion to values that define a community. In the case of friendship, the community is small. Patriotism is an example of loyalty to a larger community.

The notion that loyalty is devotion to a cause, rather than mere fidelity to the whims of an individual or organization, is one factor that distinguishes Royce's definition of loyalty from the more common "street" version of loyalty. For instance, many individuals believe that loyalty requires unwavering obedience to a given person or group, even when that person or group betrays values shared by loyalists. Roycean loyalty, on the other hand, maintains that shared values are more authoritative than individual or institutional directives. This distinction was aptly illustrated in a movie from Columbia pictures called *A Few Good Men*.

In this film, two soldiers are tried for the murder of another soldier who died while they were hazing him. In this case, the hazing consisted of a variety of humiliations and minor tortures not intended to result in permanent harm. However the victim, who was known to be a weakling, suffered unforeseen medical complications. During the trial it becomes evident that the soldiers who committed the hazing were acting on orders from their superior officer. They are acquitted of murder. Nevertheless, they are convicted of "conduct unbecoming a Marine" and discharged dishonorably from the military. Near the end of the movie, one of the Marines asks his wiser buddy how they could be convicted of wrongdoing when they were only following orders. The buddy replies: "We were supposed to fight for Freddie." Evidently, the jury believed that for Marines certain values are more authoritative than orders from a superior officer. One of these values is the notion that the strong should protect the weak. In essence, the jury affirmed the Roycean version of loyalty over crude notions of loyalty that center on following orders.

The cause, then, is a social value, shared by fellow loyalists. And loyalty is a species of devotion to such a cause. Recall that loyalty involves devotion that is "willing and practical and thoroughgoing." Royce stipulates that loyalty must be "willing" or voluntary devotion because compulsory loyalty would contradict the principle of autonomy and ruin loyalty as an ethical ideal.

This emphasis on the will of the loyalist is a feature of loyalty that commends it over the heroic ideal and the self-denying self. The hero is classically an individual who champions the predominant ethos of his culture. Royce criticized this ideal because it requires good fortune and exceptional talent. He also points out that the heroic ideal does not usually provide a sufficient emphasis on the decisional prerogative of the moral agent. It is possible to be a hero without freely choosing one's moral ideal. This difficulty is even more prominent in the self-denying self, who seeks to exhibit an utter privation of personal will.

Royce also holds that loyal devotion is practical and thoroughgoing. To be practical, loyalty must be exhibited in actions. Words and sentiments are not enough. Along with his pragmatist colleagues, Royce insists that any meaningful concept, in morality, metaphysics or elsewhere, will have practical consequences.

Loyalty is thoroughgoing in that it permeates every aspect of life. The cause is something that enthralls a loyalist. It is her constant inspiration, her plan for life. Loyalty wouldn't solve the paradox of self-realization if it demanded less. Recall that Royce defined selfhood as a "human life lived according to a plan." If he is correct, then self-realization requires a thoroughgoing ideal – one that encompasses a plan of life.

At this point Royce's reasons for endorsing loyalty over the other ideals should be apparent. Loyalty honors the principle of autonomy because it hinges on a personal decision. The loyalist chooses her causes and chooses the manner in which she will serve them. Nevertheless, unlike rebellion, loyalty also adequately reflects the social nature of moral life. The cause is not conjured by the loyalist. To the contrary, it is a thoroughly social reality. The cause is a value that structures a human community. Royce concludes that loyalty is an ideal that overcomes the paradox of self-realization.

But there is still a problem. What about loyalty to a destructive or evil cause? Some communities seem to be founded on hatred, exclusion or falsehood. Clearly Royce doesn't think that loyalty to these values is morally good. He would not commend a loyal Nazi. Perhaps the Nazi could succeed in becoming a self. But if this is so, mere selfhood does not seem to imply moral goodness. For Royce to establish that loyalty is an adequate moral ideal, he needs show us how to choose a morally acceptable cause.

Natural and Genuine Loyalty

In order to establish a criterion for estimating which causes are good and which are not so good, Royce asks us to stand back and examine what we've learned from our study of the paradox of self-realization. One lesson is that loyalty – whether to a good cause or to a bad one – is valuable for the person who is loyal:

> If… I find a cause, and this cause fascinates me, and I give myself over to its service, I in so far attain what, for me, if my loyalty is complete, is a supreme good.

A second lesson is that loyalty is good not merely for the single individual who pursues a cause. It is also good for fellow loyalists. The value of loyalty extends to all those who share a cause:

> But my cause, by our own definition, is a social cause, which binds many into the unity of one service. My cause, therefore, gives me, of necessity, fellow servants, who with me share this loyalty, and to whom this loyalty, if complete, is also a supreme good. So far, then, in being loyal myself, I not only get but give good; for I help to sustain, in each of my fellow-servants, his own loyalty, and so I help him to secure his own supreme good. In so far, then, my loyalty to my cause is also a loyalty to my fellows'

loyalty.

Loyalty seems to be good for everyone who is included in a community of loyalists. However, as we recently observed, there is a possible catch.

> But now suppose that my cause, like the family in a feud, or like the pirate ship, or like the aggressively warlike nation, lives by the destruction of the loyalty of other families, or of its own community, or of other communities. Then, indeed, I get a good for myself and for my fellow-servants by our common loyalty; but I war against this very spirit of loyalty as it appears in our opponent's loyalty to his own cause.

Royce concludes that a cause is morally good to the extent that it contributes as much as possible, and detracts as little as possible, from the loyalties of other persons.

> And so, a cause is good, not only for me, but for mankind, in so far as it is essentially a *loyalty to loyalty*, that is, is an aid and a furtherance of loyalty in my fellows. It is an evil cause in so far as, despite the loyalty it arouses in me, it is destructive of loyalty in the world of my fellows. [10]

On this basis, Royce is able to define a criterion of choice for good causes and provide basic guidance about how to formulate a life plan:

> In so far as it lies in your power, so choose your cause and so serve it, that, by reason of your choice and of your service, there shall be more loyalty in the world rather than less. And, in fact, so choose and so serve your individual cause as to secure thereby the greatest possible increase of loyalty amongst men. [11]

In *The Philosophy of Loyalty*, Royce summarizes this guidance with the rather cumbersome phrase "loyalty to loyalty." In later years, Royce sharpens his criterion for the good cause by appropriating the concept of a universal, ideal human community. We will examine this universal community in the next chapter. For now, however, it is useful to recognize that loyalty to loyalty – Royce's crowning ethical ideal – is in essence devotion to a potential community of all humanity.

The loyalist is not expected to know what such an ideal

community would be like, and is certainly not expected to create such a community within the scope of a given lifetime (or even within a finite number of lifetimes). Royce is not a utopian thinker. However loyalty, as an ethical ideal, is service that moves humanity in the direction of more harmony, of more synergy between causes, and of enhanced opportunity and inspiration for the discovery of fulfilling causes. When someone chooses and serves a cause that supports humanity in this way, Royce says her loyalty is genuine. Natural loyalties, i.e., loyalties to established communities such as families, professional groups, political organizations and religious denominations, become genuine loyalties when loyal individuals seek to serve all of humanity through their commitment to these particular communities. Genuine loyalty is the highest expression of morality, fulfilling the most fundamental needs and expressing the deepest internal meaning of the loyal individual through unique service to a universal community.

The Moral Insight

For Royce, the philosophy of loyalty is an attempt to fashion workable solutions to the problems of contemporary moral philosophy by grounding notions of duty and goodness in human experience. By examining the development of human selves and articulating the paradox of individuation, Royce hopes to focus his moral philosophy on practical problems that apply across the spectrum of human conditions. From the outset, Royce deals with a perplexing array of seemingly contradictory moral beliefs.

Conventional morality, as it is usually taught to us, consists of a maze of precepts. Some of these precepts we have acquired through the influence of Christianity. Some of them are distinctly unchristian or even antichristian. Whatever their origin, whether Christian or Greek or barbarian, they lie side by side in our minds; and sometimes they tend to come into conflict with one another. Be just; but also be kind. Be generous; but also be strict in demanding what is your due. Live for others; but also be careful of your own dignity, and assert your rights. Love all mankind; but resent insults, and be ready to slay the enemies of your country. Take no thought for the morrow; but be careful to save and to insure. Cultivate yourself; but always sacrifice yourself. [12]

In this passage Royce expresses an insight remarkably similar to the one that launches Alasdair MacIntyre's landmark late-20th-century ethical study, *After Virtue*.[13] Both Royce and MacIntyre are acutely

A typical instance of the moral insight occurs at the movies. Suppose, for instance, an American World War II veteran watches *"Das Boot,"* a film portraying the harrowing experiences of a German submarine crew. And suppose that this individual is still bitter about the many losses incurred at war; still inclined to view Germans as evil automatons; still averse to anything German. It is possible that, in the space of two hours, this jaded veteran may set aside these barriers. For a brief interlude, he may be able to view the world through the eyes of this German submarine crew – caught up in urgent decisions, longing for home, fearful and lonely. The antipathy toward Germans may be suspended. Our moviegoer may even find himself rooting for the Germans. He will provisionally will what the characters will.

When the movie ends, he will return to himself. But, insofar as he has experienced a moral insight, he will be changed. Now his thoughts about the tragedy of war will include sadness for the lost lives, the corrupted loyalties and the suffering of the Germans. He will not approve of Germany's actions; but he will understand that Germans were not wholly vicious. Perhaps it will occur to him that many Germans' deepest motives were quite the same as his own.

Similar insights often occur when we encounter other persons in unusual circumstances. These encounters can be direct or indirect, actual or imagined. The insight might come when we read a book about a Native American leader. Or when we make an emergency bivouac with a foreign climber on the slopes of Mount Adams. Perhaps spending an afternoon in detention with the class nerd (as per "The Breakfast Club") will enlighten us. Our moral insight might even occur when mother scolds us for cruelty to our little sister.

The aftermath of moral insight may be unpleasant. Moral dogmas and easy stereotypes may be challenged. The universe tends to become more complex, and moral decisions, far from being facilitated by our moral insight, may be more arduous. If the desires and aspirations of other people, even our enemies, are legitimate in some way (as the moral insight teaches), then there is much that we need to consider before passing judgment in moral issues. Hence, we are awakened to the tragic nature of human striving. For some problems there is no single acceptable solution.

Nevertheless, most of us find a degree of comfort in our moments of moral insight. We are soothed by the human contact and by the discovery of an underlying basis for unity. Further, we are ennobled by the realization that this underlying unity can be expressed in everyday life. Moral insight occurs when we observe others in the act of being loyal. Even when loyalty is directed to ideals that are stunted, selfish or shortsighted, we are able to detect their legitimacy. They are legitimate because they express humanity's deepest, common need. That is, these flawed and partial loyalties are, nonetheless, expressions of others' needs for personal identity and social integration. We are inspired to serve our local causes and, even more, to transform these causes into elements of a grander, more inclusive ideal.

Royce's moral insight is not an all-or-nothing event. It comes in degrees. It waxes, then it fades. The moral insight is a temporary and partial glimpse of the human condition. A complete and unimpeded view, on the other hand, is never obtained by finite human beings. Such clarity is reserved for the Absolute. Nevertheless, when we experience the moral insight, we align ourselves with the Absolute. We are expanded and our selfhood becomes more determinate, just as our lives enter into greater harmony with the lives of others and, ultimately, with the Absolute.

The Spirit of Loyalty

It would be a grave error to suppose that Royce's moral insight is based on sympathy or sentiment. To the contrary, provisionally taking on the will of another person requires taking on their purposes and thoughts, as well as their emotions. The moral insight is not merely affective, but also conative (dealing with intentions) and cognitive. It involves sympathy, but requires much more. Likewise, if we are to help our neighbors to live loyally, the solicitation of warm sentiments is not sufficient.

Cultivating Loyalty in Society

Royce holds that to promote loyalty on a large scale (such as a national level), it is necessary to revise our notions of philanthropy. Three elements are required. First, we should aid people in developing mental and physical powers that are necessary for expressing loyalty. Second, we should provide people with opportunities to be loyal. Third, we should show people that loyalty is their greatest good and that genuine loyalty is the highest moral ideal.

Only the first of these elements involves philanthropy in the sense that it is ordinarily understood. In order to aid people in developing mental and physical powers, it is necessary to attend to public health, education and public safety. These benefits should be provided not merely out of sympathy, but because they promote loyalty. Social services are not designed to provide fulfillment. Instead, they potentiate it. Royce holds that it is not possible to purchase human happiness through attempts to satisfy the desires of the unfulfilled. Such misguided philanthropy is more harmful than helpful. Royce writes:

> To try and deal out simple happiness to mankind at large is like persistently plying them with wine. One in so far makes them at best stupid, – perhaps even vicious.[15]

According to Royce, education, public sanitation, health care and police protection are the sorts of things that "our philanthropists and teachers and public-spirited people generally regard as important." However, Royce finds that the other two elements – providing opportunities for loyalty and examples of loyal service – are more important, yet sorely lacking in the America of his day. These objectives are impeded whenever we place too much emphasis on material success, on winning, or on simple gratification. They are also impeded by undirected pity.

> Our young people grow up with a great deal of their attention fixed upon personal success, and also with a great deal of training in sympathetic sentiments; but they get far too little knowledge, either practical or theoretical, of what loyalty means.[16]

How, then, does Royce suggest that we provide our young persons with opportunities for loyalty? And how do we instruct them on its value? Predictably, Royce answers that training in loyalty begins in the family. Royce holds that we begin to learn about loyalty when we master our familial roles – for instance, in carrying out duties of obedience to our parents and in respecting the freedom of our siblings. Our earliest instruction about right and wrong occurs within the home, and it is often other family members who introduce the heroes that capture a young imagination.

Instruction also occurs in the schools and, optimally, in a full community life involving religious activities, athletic competition, political associations and local traditions. Royce endorses "wise provincialism," which consists in regional devotion that is based not on racial or ethnic pride, nor on a sense of cultural superiority, but which derives from the conviction that a thriving community life, full of local symbols and customs, is a concrete good, worthy of affection and allegiance. Though Royce was always wary about the shortsighted provincialism he witnessed in the California of his youth, he later became equally wary of the "leveling effect" of a national mass media, which may facilitate an even more pernicious form of mindless conformity, such as we see in belligerent nationalism and ethnic cleansing. Mob spirit, it seems, is possible on large and on small scales. The best defense against it, according to the mature Royce, is the provincialism of genuinely loyal persons.

> Enlightened loyalty, as we have learned, means harm to no man's loyalty. It is at war only with disloyalty, and its warfare, unless necessity constrains, is only a spiritual warfare. It does not foster class hatreds; it knows of nothing reasonable about race prejudices, and it regards all races of men as one in their need of loyalty.[17]

> We need and we are beginning to get, in this country, a new and wiser provincialism. I mean by such provincialism no mere renewal of the old sectionalism. I mean the sort of provincialism which makes people want to idealize, to adorn, to ennoble, to educate, their own province; to hold sacred its traditions, to honor its worthy dead, to support and to multiply its public possessions. I mean the spirit which shows itself in the multiplying of public libraries, in the laying out of public parks, in the work of local historical societies...[18]

Conscience

We have observed that Royce's theory of loyalty solves the paradox of self-realization and provides the basis for a psychologically adequate personality ideal. We have examined Royce's method for selecting a worthy cause and learned that this method supports and is supported by the moral (and metaphysical) insight that human beings are connected. Finally, we have looked at the ways in which loyalty is promoted in society at large. Next, we will consider how Roycean loyalty helps the moral agent to make difficult moral decisions.

Royce believes that we must appeal to our conscience when we are faced with challenging moral decisions. This leads, of course, to questions about the nature of conscience:

> What is conscience? You will agree that the word names a mental possession of ours which enables us to pass some sort of judgment, correct or mistaken, upon moral questions as they arise. My conscience, then, belongs to my mental equipment, and tells me about right and wrong conduct... Our differences regarding our conscience begin when questions arise of the following sort: Is our conscience inborn? Is it acquired by training? Are the dictates the same in all men? Is it God-given? Is it infallible? Is it

a separate power of the mind? Or is it simply a name for a collection of habits that we have acquired through social training, through reasoning, and through personal experience of the consequences of conduct?[19]

Royce has some rather definite answers to these questions. First, conscience is not inborn. The desire for meaning and personal identity, on the other hand, is the stimulus for developing a conscience, and this desire is our natural inheritance. Second, conscience is acquired through the process of cultivating a personal ideal. Third, the dictates of conscience are not the same in all people. Conscience, even when it is healthy and fully formed, will be a product of each individual's unique experience, reflecting her unique personality. Fourth, conscience is God-given in the sense that it is purposeful. Recall that each of our internal meanings is an expression of the divine purpose. However, conscience is not God-given in the sense that it reflects particular determinations of our own conscious will that are not handed down by God. Fifth, conscience is an expression of human judgment, and human judgments are always fallible. Even the most highly developed human conscience will be prone to error. Sixth, conscience is not a separate power or faculty of the mind. To the contrary, it is our deepest will insofar as we have been able to elucidate it. Finally, conscience is indeed partially constituted by habits – especially habits of thought – that we have acquired through training, reasoning and experience. But conscience is no passive consequence. It is not merely a result of our experience. To the contrary, it shapes experience. There is a continuous feedback loop between our conscience and the actions and experiences it funds.

Royce believes that conscience is the inner voice of our loyalties. It is a manifestation of our cause. Royce writes:

> My cause, then, for our philosophy of loyalty, *is* my conscience, – my cause as interpreted through my ideal of my personal life. When I look to my cause, it furnishes me with a conscience; for it sets before me a plan or ideal of life, and then constantly bids me contrast this plan, this ideal, with my transient and momentary impulses. [20]

Moral dilemmas occur, on Royce's account, when loyalties conflict. Though he sometimes writes about the cause as if it were a simple unity, Royce is aware that each of us will have numerous causes and, hence, numerous loyalties. These causes coalesce into a unified personal cause or life plan that is of necessity rather complex.

Moral doubts arise in the loyal mind when there is an apparent conflict between loyalties. As a fact, that cause, which in any sense unifies a life as complex as my human life is, must of course be no perfectly simple cause. By virtue of my nature and of my social training, I belong to a family, to a community, to a calling, to a state, to humanity. In order to be loyal to loyalty, and in order to be a person at all, I must indeed unify my loyalty. In the meantime, however, I must also choose special causes to serve; and if these causes are to interest me, if they are to engross and to possess me, they must be such as together appeal to many diverse sides of my nature; they must involve me in numerous and often conflicting social tasks; they can form one cause only so far as they constitute an entire system of causes. [21]

Does conscience provide us with a means for navigating the conflicts between (or, I would add, even within) our various causes? Sometimes the answer is clearly "No." The agonizing nature of certain moral dilemmas is evidence enough that our conscience offers no clear guidance on these issues. Royce believes, in fact, that moral agonies of this sort will never be fully eradicated.

On the other hand, Royce holds that his theory of loyalty provides necessary guidance to tutor our conscience in case of such moral dilemmas. This guidance consists, in part, of two additional rules of loyalty. First, we should be decisive. It is not permissible to delay moral decisions to the point that the delay becomes a moral decision by default. As time permits, we should deliberate intensely about important decisions. Perhaps we can list pros and cons. But ultimately we must reach some kind of internal or external consensus. We must harmonize our loyalties as well as our current understanding allows.

Second, we should stick to our decisions unless there is new and compelling evidence that we are mistaken. When we reach a difficult moral decision, we formulate a plan of action. This new plan becomes part of our cause. Vacillation is not conducive to loyal service.

Only a growth in knowledge which makes it evident that the special cause once chosen is an unworthy cause, disloyal to universal loyalty, – only such a growth in knowledge can absolve from fidelity to the cause once chosen. [22]

In the end, Royce's philosophy of loyalty offers no release from

The problem with the entities of critical rationalism is that they lack individuality. Valid judgments, according to Royce, are always judgments about possible experience and, hence, cannot explain the individual. Even particular judgments are ultimately only judgments about possible experience. For instance, "Socrates is mortal" does not explain the unique meaning or essence of Socrates. It tells us only that Socrates belongs to the class of things that will die. Further, "Socrates is mortal" and "Socrates will die next Tuesday" do not foretell a specific human experience – that is, they don't describe Socrates' death as it is, essentially – but instead negatively delineate a realm of possible human experiences. They tell us that Socrates, whatever he is, will not be playing tennis next Thursday. Even the vast totality of valid particular judgments about Socrates will not explain Socrates as an individual. The "is" in these judgments is always that of predication, not identity. And predication is never enough to explain the being of individuals. Particulars, then, are not fully individuals. Particulars are the objects of judgments, and judgments point only to a realm of possible confirmation or fulfillment. Individuals are actually fulfilled judgments or ideas.

Royce's objection to critical rationalism may be easier to comprehend when viewed from an ethical frame of reference. Ethically speaking, our internal meanings are our purposes, which is to say that they are the causes we serve. It is not enough, Royce holds, that the universe provides a possible fulfillment of these purposes. The fulfillment – i.e., the Great Community – must be real. But the reality of such an infinite, universal community requires an absolute consciousness. Royce's "Fourth Conception of Being" is reality conceived as a fully determinate idea of this absolute consciousness. Absolute idealism, then, is for Royce the only adequate conception of being.

Bradley's Objection

F.H. Bradley, another absolute idealist of Royce's day, held that the human mind is incapable of grasping the unity between finite individuals and the Absolute. In *Appearance and Reality*, Bradley argues that we live in a realm of Appearance and that reason cannot give a fully adequate account of the relationship between Appearance and Reality (Reality being the realm of the Absolute).[9] Every attempt to express a relationship between the Absolute and a finite individual results in a particular mediating idea (i.e., an idea that relates the individual to the Absolute). Let us designate an instance of such a mediating idea with the term "R." Now, in order to bring our synthesis

54

of Appearance and Reality to completion, we will have to offer an account of the relation between this mediating idea, R, and the Absolute. Hence, we will have to offer another mediating idea, R', that relates R to the Absolute. But then we will need to explain how R' is related to the Absolute. This will require a third mediating idea, R'', which will in turn require another mediating idea, R''', and so forth. We will be led into an infinite regress. Since Bradley believes the concept of such an infinite fission of ideas is self-contradictory, he holds that it is impossible to conceive of a relationship between finite individuals and the Absolute. In other words, Bradley claims that Royce's "fourth conception" is not a conception at all, because it involves us in the self-contradictory activity of defining an actual infinite.

Royce clearly acknowledges that if it is impossible to conceive of an actual infinite, then his fourth conception of being must give way to something like Bradley's mystical account of the relationship between the Absolute and the finite. But Royce is too much a rationalist to accept Bradley's position. He is also too much a classic metaphysician to accept Hegel's bungling, romantic disregard for mathematics. In order to overcome Bradley's objection, Royce appeals to a mathematician, Richard Dedekind. Dedekind's conception of an infinite, self-representative series appears in Royce's initial rejoinder to Bradley, published in his "Supplementary Essay" at the conclusion of the first volume of *The World and the Individual*.[10]

The Self-Representative Series

Bradley holds that the aforementioned infinite explanatory regress is an inevitable result of any attempt to unify Appearance and Reality because the ground of unity is external to finite thought. But Royce views the situation differently, holding that many diverse concepts are organically united by the singular purpose of human thought:

> If the diversities were complementary aspects of a process of connection and distinction, the process not being external to the elements, or, again, a foreign compulsion of the intellect, but itself the intellect's own *proprius motus*, the case would be altered. Each aspect would of itself be a transition to the other aspect, a transition intrinsic and natural at once to itself, and to the intellect.[11]

It is quite evident that Royce is struggling here to articulate something like the theory of interpretation (with its doctrine of the inherent continuity in thought) that he will develop after his study of of unfolding purposes cannot be easily linked with a series of distinctions. The former series, in the World of Appreciation, seems to fit nicely with Royce's account of an infinite self-representative series. The conceptual distinctions of the World of Description, on the other hand, seem to form a different kind of series – a dense series – that, mathematically speaking, cannot be linked in an orderly way with the elements of a self-representative series.

The mathematical intricacies of this problem are beyond our scope. Nevertheless, it is easy to illustrate the manner in which a dense series, created by an infinite series of conceptual distinctions, differs from a self-representative series. Suppose we have a line segment between two points, A and B. And suppose we divide segment AB into two segments, AC and CB. Both AC and CB are capable of further divisions. For instance, AC may be divided into AD and DC. AD, in turn, may be divided into AE and ED, and so forth. It is possible to continue this process of division infinitely. A series of such divisions is called a dense series, since the space between A and B is fixed and apparently finite, but it contains an infinite number of distinguishable segments.

Royce accepts (with Aristotle, Bradley and many other reputable metaphysicians) that a series of conceptual distinctions is a kind of dense series. We begin with two concepts and select a mediating concept – which is a concept that lies, metaphorically speaking, between the initial concepts. However, in order to explain how the mediating concept is related to each of the two initial concepts, we require another mediating concept, and so forth. The series of distinctions can proceed interminably, yet the ultimate boundaries of these distinctions are fixed by the initial concepts. Unfortunately, the order exhibited in such a dense series cannot be replicated in the description of a self-representative series. The World of Appreciation, then, seems to be permanently sundered (rather than provisionally sundered, as Royce claims in *The World and the Individual*) from the World of Description.[17]

In order to overcome this difficulty, Royce struggles for several years after *The World and the Individual* to define a new theory of order. Eventually he describes System Sigma. Though it is beyond our scope to examine Sigma in detail, we need to recognize certain characteristics of this theory of order to appreciate Royce's synthesis of the World of Appreciation and the World of Description and form a basic understanding of Royce's mature philosophy of God.

System Sigma

A theory of order, such as Sigma, is a theory about the most fundamental ways of organizing concepts. According to Royce, the various conceptual schemes we apply in symbolic logic, mathematics, physics, zoology, ethics, natural theology and all other domains of rational inquiry are particular instances or interpretations of a general theory of order.

Royce, like Peirce, was a student of logician Alfred Bray Kempe. Kempe described his "base system" or theory of order in terms of a so-called "F-relation." The F-relation is a general "between" relation, such as we find in a dense series of conceptual distinctions, where each new mediating idea is located somewhere "between" the concepts it mediates.[18] Royce replaced Kempe's F-relation with the O-relation, which is more basic because it includes an infinite variety of polyadic relations (relations including various numbers of terms) rather than just dyadic (two term) or triadic (three term) relations. The O-relation is the fundamental relation in Sigma

In addition to a conception of the O-relation, Sigma also contains conceptions of (1) class, (2) series and (3) operation. The notion of "class" requires a concept of an element, object or individual, which Royce says will be determined in each specific field by the purposes of inquiry (recall Royce's earlier description of individuals as objects of exclusive attention). It also requires a concept of membership, a concept of assertion (which declares "that an object is or is not a member of a given class) and a normative concept that enables us to decide which of these assertions are true and which are false."[19] As Royce observed in his account of self-representative series, the purpose that defines individual members of a class may also be used as an operator to define a series.

Royce interprets the universe as an expression of Sigma. The O-relation, on this account, is the property found in the most fundamental act of conceptual mediation. It is the "yes-no" relation, which pertains in dyadic judgments of true or not-true, good or not-good, etc., and in polyadic judgments such as a selection between many colors. Working from his pragmatist insight that ideas are plans for action, Royce identifies the O-relation as a relation between possible attitudes of the will. Each attitude of will is a mode of action that generates a class or series of possible interpretations. The universe is an infinite series generated by God's will, which is a fundamental mode of action. This infinite series contains an array of sub-series, each defined by modes of action that are determined in various ways by the fundamental, divine higher persons. The life plan in Royce's mature thought makes the same metamorphosis as the cause. It becomes both forward looking and responsive to the past.

Triune God

Any viable religious community will embody the spirit of genuine loyalty. That is, it will be constituted, in each member as well as in its wholeness, by devotion to a universal community. Combining this insight with his notion of the Absolute, and with mature reflections about the nature of community, Royce develops his notion of the Beloved Community.

In *The Problem of Christianity*, Royce's Absolute evolves from a totality of consciousness into an infinite community of interpretation. In this work, reference to the Absolute practically ceases, being replaced by a triune of Beloved Community (God as the highest individual), Redeemer (God as atoning symbol) and Holy Spirit (God as the immanent will to interpret). In the remainder of this chapter, we will briefly examine each element of his holy Trinity. In what follows, it is important to realize that Royce does not assume the rightness of Christianity. Nor is he a Christian apologist. *The Problem of Christianity* is merely Royce's attempt to express fundamental metaphysical and ethical insights in terms of Christian symbols. Whether or not such a task is feasible is, for Royce, "the problem" of Christianity. For the purposes of this volume, a brief overview of Royce's doctrine of the Trinity is helpful because it illustrates aspects of his mature metaphysical and ethical thought.

God as Universal Community

The first element of the Trinity is the universal community. This is an ideal community that harmonizes the manifold causes of all the genuinely loyal and which includes all persons just because genuine loyalty is the deepest object of every personal will. From the Christian perspective, this universal community is the ideal church (conceived here as the ideal community insofar as it can be expressed through Christian symbols). The visible church, on the other hand, is a concrete expression, limited and quite fallible, of this ideal church.

As we have noted, Royce's universal community is also called the Beloved Community. In fact it has many names. In order to avoid confusion, it helps to recognize that each of the various terms for the universal community is selected to highlight certain aspects of Royce's ideal community. In general, Royce uses "Beloved Community" when he is discussing the universal community in a religious context and

"Great Community" in political or humanitarian contexts. The term "genuine community" is used to designate any community that is consciously integrated with the universal community.

When Royce speaks about the ideal community in the present tense, as if it exists today, he means to highlight that (1) every human person is a member of the universal community insofar as it is the fulfillment of her deepest personal will and an expression of her personal identity in its most extended sense, and (2) visible communities are also elements of the ideal community, since they are types of person that also can be fulfilled only through the universal community. In these two senses, the ideal community does exist today. In another sense, the ideal community, like Royce's earlier version of the Absolute, transcends the temporal manifold.

Working from Royce's notion that communities are persons, it follows that the universal community is also a person, namely the person who fulfills every purpose in a single life. This person is God, according to Royce. God is the fully determinate person who actualizes the ideal community in an infinite process of interpretation. Like Royce's Absolute, God as an infinite, universal community cannot be fully comprehended by a finite thinker or a finite community.

Atonement

Before we can understand Royce's mature interpretation of God or complete our survey of Royce's response to the problem of evil, it is necessary to examine his doctrine of atonement. For Royce, atonement is a necessary component of any mature moral outlook, whether it is Christian or not.

> The human aspect of the Christian idea of atonement is based upon such motives that, if there were no Christianity and no Christians in the world, the idea of atonement would have to be invented, before the higher levels of our moral existence could be fairly understood.[33]

The idea of atonement is a response to one aspect of the problem of evil – namely the problem of original sin or, in Royce's words, "the moral burden of the individual." Unlike John Stuart Mill, who held that social cohesiveness is a product of advanced culture, Royce believes that solidarity is more difficult to achieve in large, highly evolved communities than it is in smaller, more primitive ones. The advanced society will have a richer community life, but it will also be more complex and more susceptible to corruption, alienation and treachery.

69

Royce believes that evolving persons – whether they be individuals or communities – experience a moral burden just insofar as they incur, with each level of progress, more opportunities to betray their loyalties and, inevitably, failure to serve their causes in a thoroughgoing sense.

This moral burden crystallizes in the problem of the traitor. Two conditions are required to create a traitor:

> The first condition is that a traitor is a man who has had an ideal, and who has lived it with all his heart and his soul and his mind and his strength. His ideal must have seemed to him to furnish the cause of his life. It must have meant to him what Paul meant by the grace that saves. He must have embraced it, for the time, with full loyalty. It must have been his religion, his way of salvation. It must have been the cause of a Beloved Community.[34]

The second condition is that the traitor must have betrayed his cause. In some voluntary act, he must have been deliberately false to it. This infidelity, even if it were to occur once only, leaves the traitor in what Royce calls, "the hell of the irrevocable." The past cannot be undone and hence the traitor must live out his life with knowledge of his treason.

Not only is betrayal a burden for the traitor, it also permanently scars the community which he endeavors to loyally serve.

> But what is indeed irrevocably lost to the community through the traitor's deed is precisely what I just called 'unscarred love.' The traitor remains – for the community as well as for himself – the traitor,– just so far as his deed is confessed, and just so far as his once unsullied fidelity has been stained. *This* indeed is irrevocable. It is perfectly human. But it is unutterably comfortless to the shattered community.[35]

All human beings are frail. For Royce, this perfectly human characteristic is the only sensible interpretation of original sin. That is, original sin is the moral burden inevitably incurred by each individual when we betray our loyalties. The question of evil arises again. Why have we been created to be so fallible? In what sense is our world so grand if error and betrayal constantly shatter it?

This leads Royce to the notion of atonement or reconciliation. For Royce, reconciliation cannot be achieved by restoring loyalty, or by forgiveness. A creative act is required. Some third party, other than the traitor or the aggrieved, must imagine and carry out a work of love such that the community is enriched, ennobled and improved – so that the community is somehow better than it was before the betrayal.

> When treason has done its last and most cruel work, and lies with what it has destroyed,– dead in the tomb of the irrevocable past,– there is now the opportunity for a triumph of which I can only speak weakly and in imperfectly abstract formulas. But, as I can at once say, this of which I now speak is a human triumph. It forms part of the history of man's earthly warfare with his worst foes. Moreover, whenever it occurs at all, this is a triumph, *not* merely of stoical endurance, nor yet of kindly forgiveness, nor of the mystical mood which, seeing all things in God, feels them all to be good. It is a triumph of the creative will.[36]

This triumph can be achieved only through the agency of a loyal individual "who acts, so to speak, as the incarnation of the very spirit of community itself." The highest calling, for any loyal individual of any creed, is to embody this spirit of redemption in creative service. For the Christian, such loyalty is exemplified, at it highest level, in the life of Jesus Christ.

God as Redeemer

Royce's Christology is deceptively simple, yet luxuriantly rich in its implications. Christ is, for Royce, an enduring, living, growing symbol of Christian love, especially as that love is creatively expressed in acts of atonement.

> Christian religious feeling has always expressed itself in the idea that what atones is something perfectly "objective," namely, Christ's work. And this atoning work of Christ was for Christian feeling a deed that was made possible only through man's sin, but that somehow was so wise and so rich and so beautiful and divinely fair that, after this work was done, the world was a better world than it would have been had *man* never sinned.[37]

Royce is insistent that Christ's work is an ongoing reality. Redemption is not a finished product, fully completed during the life of Jesus. To the contrary, it is the risen Christ – the Christ of Pauline Christianity and the Christ who animates the Beloved Community in its contemporary form – who offers hope for a fulfilling future. Atonement is a creative act that is not effected by reciting historical events. Though Christianity is founded, in part, as a community of memory, faithfully interpreting the deeds of the historical Jesus, it is also a community of hope. Interpretation is not merely recollection; it is also creation. Christ is the symbol of the interpretive spirit of Christianity.

Other religious communities (and non-religious ones as well) will have their own symbols of atonement. From a purely theoretical standpoint, outside Christianity, Royce's doctrine of God as Redeemer seems to be the doctrine that any viable orientation to the universal community will require compelling, living symbols that convert the community of memory into a dynamic, forward-looking entity.

God as Interpreter-Spirit

Moral burdens apply to communities as well as individuals. Natural communities, left to their finite, human resources, are doomed to fail. They miss the truth. They misunderstand neighboring communities. They persecute the innocent. They wallow thoughtlessly in stagnant dogmas. They partition themselves into sects and they construct divisive hierarchies, thus creating both external and internal forms of alienation. Like human individuals, natural communities are lost without help from God.

As we have noted, Royce believes that some help comes through the atoning work of Christ. According to Royce's version of Christian theology, Christ's work is the concrete form, the embodiment of a universal spirit of interpretation that graces the Beloved Community and enlightens every individual consciousness. This spirit, in its universal form, is the Roycean version of the Holy Spirit. Royce's general (non-Christianized) term for this aspect of God is "Interpreter-Spirit."

The Interpreter-Spirit is what binds members of the Beloved Community through grace. It is the divine spark that constitutes our internal meanings, ignites our will to interpret, and guides us gradually towards truth and fulfillment.

Theologically speaking, the Interpreter-Spirit is perhaps most significant as the instrument of grace by which divine revelation becomes possible. In *Sources of Religious Insight*, Royce asks, how is revelation possible? How do we recognize God's authentic word, as opposed to some attractive counterfeit? His answer is that God is immanent in each individual as the spirit of interpretation. Recall that Royce's Absolute was the source of our deepest will. Recall also that Royce identified genuine loyalty as the fullest human expression of this deepest will. Now see how these provide the basis for an account of revelation. When we are genuinely loyal, we live in the spirit of God's purpose, of our deepest will, and in this spirit we are able to recognize the difference between divine inspiration and mere sentimentality. The universal community becomes our extended self. In essence, Royce believes that the Beloved Community is a graced community, just insofar as the spirit of genuine loyalty animates it, and just insofar as this spirit of loyalty is an expression of divine purpose.

Grace is a salutary, not only as a means for spiritual progress, but also, in a broader sense, as the ultimate source of insight in the arts, humanities and sciences.[38] Grace and its bearer, the Interpreter Spirit, is the true spirit of loyalty, animating human inquiry as it provides hope that each individual life will reach an ultimate fulfillment. Likewise, the Holy Trinity represents three elements that are present in any process of inquiry – community, sign and interpreter. God is a fully determinate expression of all three elements.

Endnotes

1. PL, 166.
2. Natural theology is the study of God, undertaken without reliance on divine revelation.
3. WI:I, 11.
4. WI:I, 16.
5. WI:I, 22-23.
6. WI:I, 62
7. WI:I, 83
8. WI:I, 202-203
9. Francis Herbert Bradley, *Appearance and Reality* (London: Macmillan, 1893).
10. WI:I, 507-512.
11. WI:I, 488.
12. Such mathematical aspirations, as Peirce observes in his review of *The World and the Individual*, are not inconsistent with the theory of interpretation. However, at Peirce's behest, Royce undertakes a study of logic that leads to changes in his theory of order.
13. WI:I, 495-496.
14. WI:I, 518.
15. WI:I, 509.
16. WI:II, 2-26.
17. For a detailed description of this difficulty, see Bruce Kuklick, *Josiah Royce: An Intellectual Biography* (Indianapolis: Hackett, 1985), 137-153.
18. Alfred B. Kempe, "On the Relation between the Logical Theory of Classes and the Geometrical Theory of Points,"

Proceedings of the London Mathematical Society 21 (1890): 147-182.

19. Josiah Royce, *Royce's Logical Essays*, ed. Daniel S. Robinson (Dubuque, Iowa: Wm. C. Brown Company, 1951), 349. Royce's emphases are deleted. Hereafter this book will be abbreviated RLE.

20. Kuklick, 199-203.

21. The doctrine of freedom in the World of Appreciation, as here understood, is compatible with a deterministic account of causation in the World of Description. See WI:II, 323-331.

22. RLE, 390. See also Oppenheim, 57.

23. Josiah Royce, *Studies of Good and Evil* (New York: D. Appleton and Company, 1898), 2; PJR, 85-86. Hereafter, *Studies of Good and Evil* will be abbreviated SGE.

24. SGE, 7; PJR, 90.

25. SGE, 13-14; PJR, 95.

26. SGE, 23; PJR, 102.

27. It is not clear how an all-knowing God can experience our despair, since despair seems at times predicated on an inability to appreciate "the big picture." Perhaps Royce needs to concede that the way the Absolute experiences our despair is analogous to the way in which a parent suffers the anguish of a child. The parent may be aware that the particular suffering is necessary or temporary, but nonetheless suffers acutely out of empathy. See Gabriel Marcel, *Royce's Metaphysics* (Chicago: Henry Regnery Co., 1956), p. 82.

28. SGE, 24; PJR, 103.

29. Josiah Royce, "Immortality," in *William James and Other Essays on the Philosophy of Life* (New York: Macmillan, 1911), 257-298. This essay was initially delivered as an address in 1906. Hereafter, *William James and Other Essays on the Philosophy of Life* will be abbreviated WJ.

30. Clendenning, 296.

31. Søren Kierkegaard, "Fear and Trembling," in *Fear and Termbling and Sickness Unto Death*, trans. Walter Lowrie (Princeton, New Jersey: Princeton University Press, 1954), 21-132.

32. Josiah Royce, *The Problem of Christianity* (Chicago: University of Chicago Press, 1968 [1918]), 248. Hereafter, this book will be abbreviated PC.

33. PC, 165.

34. PC, 168.

35. PC, 177.
36. PC, 179-180.
37. PC, 185.
38. Royce's account of the role of the Interpreter-Spirit in the advancement of the sciences is influenced by Peirce's discussion in "A Neglected Argument for the Reality of God." See Charles Sanders Peirce, *The Essential Peirce: Selected Philosophical Writings*, Vol. 2, ed. Peirce Edition Project (Bloomington and Indianapolis: Indiana University Press, 1998), 434-450.

4

The Community of Inquiry

The Will to Interpret

The will to interpret is manifested in every characteristic form of human activity. According to Royce, it is the vivifying impulse at work not only in religious interpretation, but also in scientific, artistic, philosophical and political inquiry. In the current chapter we will explore loyalty as it occurs in these secular realms. We will also examine some of the important ways in which Charles Sanders Peirce influenced the mature Royce.

Peirce argued that three sentiments are necessary for any process of inquiry: (1) "interest in an indefinite community," (2) "recognition of the possibility of this interest being made supreme," and (3) "hope in the unlimited continuance of intellectual activity." Inquiry proceeds by way of inference – that is, by a process of reasoning from premises or experiences to conclusions. Peirce held that, since inference is based on probability, no inference is secure except when every possibility has been exhausted. But this implies that inquiry must be infinite and also that it must be social. Peirce writes:

(D)eath makes the number of our risks, of our inferences, finite, and so makes their mean result uncertain. The very idea of probability and of reasoning rests on the assumption that this number is indefinitely great... It seems to me that we are driven to this, that logicality inexorably requires that our interests shall *not* be limited. They must not stop at our own fate, but must embrace the whole community. This community, again, must not be limited, but must extend to all races of beings with whom we can come into immediate or mediate intellectual relation. It must reach, however vaguely, beyond this geological epoch, beyond all bounds. He who would not sacrifice his own soul to save the whole world, is, as it seems to me, illogical in all his inferences, collectively. Logic is rooted in the social principle.[1]

Peirce's logician's creed here sounds very much like Royce's doctrine of genuine loyalty. Hope for the realization of an infinite community of inquiry is, for Peirce, a postulate of logic and a prerequisite for any coherent notion of truth. As we have seen, Royce agrees. Both thinkers also agree that for the community of inquiry to succeed, it must be directed toward the truth. This is where the will to interpret comes into play.

Peirce's three sentiments – interest in the infinite community, recognition that this interest can guide inquiry, and hope for the realization of such a community – are required, but they are not enough to bring success. Hope must be founded on reality. There must be an actual basis for finding truth in inquiry. For Royce, this basis is the presence of the Interpreter-Spirit which guides human progress and inquiry. The eternal and infinite truth is accessible (though never fully comprehended) for finite humanity just because it is expressed in the internal meaning of every individual inquirer.

The will to interpret is the immanent Interpreter-Spirit and it is the ultimate source of Royce's ontology of persons (ontology being a set of claims about what exists). The will to interpret, then, is not merely a wish for truth. It is the germ of truth within each inquirer, seeking to actualize itself through a fundamentally social process of interpretation. Understood in this way, Royce's theory of inquiry is an account of self-discovery in community.

On the other hand, Peirce struggles to explain the success of inquiry because he defines truth as inquiry's final outcome. This is satisfactory, as far as it goes, but it does not explain how truth can guide present inquiry. For this purpose, it is not enough to conceive truth as a property of the long run. It must also be present in the here-and-now.

Like Peirce, Royce ultimately constructs his theory of inquiry on the basis of a sign-cognitive account of reality. Let us now turn to this account.

The Doctrine of Signs

An interpretive process will contain three elements: (1) something interpreted, (2) an interpreter, and (3) something towards which the interpreter and the thing interpreted aim. Four our purposes, these elements will be called, respectively, the principal, the interpreter and the interpretant. As we shall see, each of these elements is a sign, i.e., something that stands for something to something else.[2]

The following examples of interpretive process my help illustrate this terminology. First consider a literature professor who explains *Go Down Moses* to her students. Here the book is a principal, the professor is an interpreter, and her words, as well as the comprehending thoughts of the students are interpretants. Subsequent words, thoughts and acts of the students which are motivated, in part, by their recollection of this book are also interpretants of *Go Down Moses* though they may be, at the same time, interpretants of other signs as well. The object of a sign (i.e., what it interprets) may be very complex. Second, consider the case of a motorist who stops at a stop sign. In this case, the traffic engineer's plan to have people stop at this location is a principal, the stop sign an interpreter and the action of the motorist (stopping his car) an interpretant. Another way of describing the same event is to say that the stop sign is a principal, the driver an interpreter, and his action the interpretant. The stop sign in this example is both a principal and an interpreter. A single sign can (and usually does) perform many functions at once.

Note that the interpreter and the terminus of interpretation, the interpretant, may themselves be interpreted. Hence, every sign is potentially a principal; signs are entities that can be interpreted. Note also that complexes of signs may be interpreted. In fact, the universe is, for Peirce and Royce, a complex of signs that is a unity – a single sign – just insofar as it can be interpreted. Royce holds, additionally, that human beings, communities and the universe are each complex signs that become increasingly complex as they interpret themselves.

This doctrine of signs (or "semiotics") is a powerful tool Royce uses to explain and enrich several of his fundamental philosophical commitments. We will explore this dimension of the mature Royce by reexamining his notions of consciousness, of community and of loyalty in light of this doctrine of signs.

The Semiotic Account of Consciousness

According to Peirce, every thought is a sign that interprets an antecedent thought-sign. Thought-signs have an intrinsic character and a representative character. The objective or representative character of thought-signs consists of the manner in which they interpret antecedent signs to future signs. The intrinsic character, on the other hand, is fleeting and unreflective.

Another example may be helpful here. Consider the case of a midnight stroll. Jim wakes up from a sound sleep and heads toward the bathroom. Suddenly, he experiences a searing sensation in his left foot. This sensation is very intense, so that it pushes aside his thoughts about bathroom-going. Let us designate Jim's experience at this instance with the symbol S1 (Sign #1). First note that our dictum "every thought is a sign that interprets an antecedent thought-sign" is challenged by this example. The overriding characteristic of S1 is the searing sensation, which arises unexpectedly and is not an interpretation of a previous thought. Nevertheless, Royce would hold that the interpretive stream that was unfolding prior to the unexpected pain continues in the painful thought, though it is at this point not an object of Jim's conscious attention. The fact that we can remember earlier thoughts and events long after our attention has been diverted elsewhere is evidence that Royce is right here. Hence, S1 interprets Jim's previous thoughts even though it is predominately an unexpected, unanalyzed feeling. In the very next instant, the searing sensation, which may already be decreasing in intensity, becomes the object of interpretation. Jim says (or thinks) "Ouch," thus interpreting (in S2) the sensation as pain. The complex of S1-S2 may then become the object of S3, Jim's thought: "I've stepped on one of Joseph's toys." Of course, this thought may be interpreted in numerous ways – by TV restrictions for Joseph, by Jim's decision to turn on the light the next time he goes to the bathroom at night, etc.

This example is interesting in that it gives a triadic, interpretive account of an event that is commonly taken as a paradigm case of a dyadic (stimulus and response) process. Jim's exclamation, "Ouch," has a voluntary element on Royce's account, whereas it is wholly involuntary according to the behaviorist who employs the stimulus-response model. Though Royce agrees that "Ouch" may be rather automatic in this case, he also holds that it reflects Jim's prior experience, not only in learning the English language and feeling pain, but also in deciding on the proper response to unexpected pain. It would be possible, for instance if Jim were to devote himself to the doctrine of stoicism, to develop a different response to searing sensations. Or, if Jim were a crude sort, he might have programmed himself to utter an expletive rather than the inoffensive "Ouch." Royce's account seems to be superior to behaviorism, insofar as it incorporates the behaviorist's insights while also explaining why we consider ourselves responsible for our habits and for momentarily unreflective acts that express these habits. It would be no surprise to find that semiotics outshines behaviorism in explaining complex cognitive acts. However, when it exceeds behaviorism in matters such as Jim's toy stepping, we have impressive evidence that it is widely applicable. In fact, interpretation has been used as an explanatory scheme even for non-sentient events.

Peirce held, and Royce eventually agreed, that reality is semiotic in nature. That is, everything that exists is a sign. A wooden chair, for instance, is an individual thing (as Royce remarked early in his middle period) because we interpret it as such. Peirce adds that there is a semiotic character that exists within the chair, apart from our specific interpretation.[3]

Perhaps Royce and Peirce never wholly converged in their accounts of physical objects. However, both thinkers view the external world as an embodied sequence of interweaving signs that exhibits a manner of being that is distinct from the finite consciousness of human interpreters. Further, each holds that physical objects are manifestations of mind and that the essence of mind is purposefulness. Hence, Royce and Peirce are both teleologists (they believe that reality is ultimately purposeful).

For Royce, the externality of physical reality consists of the manner in which our descriptions of it always elude our purposes. That is, our internal meanings and external meanings never quite hook up. In terms of the language of semiotics, the external nature of physical objects resides in the fact that they are never fully and determinately interpreted by an individual human thought-sign. If we were to extend our thoughts infinitely, we would eventually come to experience physical objects as fulfillments of conscious purposes, rather than as independent, external objects.

Consciousness is a peculiar attribute of certain signs. It is the mode that expresses thought. Hence, it cannot be attributed to physical objects. Neither Royce nor Peirce thinks that a chair or a plant (or even a bird) can think. Like all semiotic processes, consciousness is characterized by the existence of purposes. It is distinguished from other forms of mental life by the phenomenon of self-regulation. On this, Peirce and Royce clearly agree. Peirce writes that "the function of consciousness is to render self-control possible and efficient."[4] As we have seen, Royce believes that the purpose of consciousness is to formulate and carry out a plan.

Royce and Peirce also agree that self-regulation is a social rather than an introspective process. Self-regulation is purposeful integration between internal and external aspects of experience. The external aspects, to which the internal consciousness adapts or conforms, are largely social influences. Royce also subscribed to the Peircean doctrine that there is no immediate perception of the self (i.e., no power of introspection). Instead, self-consciousness is an interpretation or inference, based on our experience of external reality. Infants, for instance, have a psychological life but no concept of self. They experience reality holistically. Only after an extensive web of interpretations (imitations and oppositions) do they develop even the most rudimentary notion of individuality or selfhood.

To say that the development of the self is social is not to infer that the self cannot be directed by an immanent will to interpret. For Peirce, will is largely a manifestation of what he calls "Secondness," which is an experience of confrontation between habits or purposes and aspects of the external world that oppose these habits or purposes. Doubt, for instance, is the result of such a confrontation between beliefs (which are habits of thought) and certain experiences that call these beliefs into question. For Royce, this account of the will as Secondness adequately explains the superficial will. The deeper will, on the other hand, is the more primordial purposeful nature of cognition. It is the will to interpret. According to Royce's theory of interpretation, this will to interpret cannot be examined directly. Instead, it manifests itself through a process of inquiry. That is, it stimulates inquiry while also being the ultimate object of inquiry.

The lack of a power of introspection or direct access to the self is also exhibited in Royce's account of the paradox of individuation. It is impossible to discover the self's deepest will or authentic values by looking inward. Hence, Royce's theory of consciousness, largely shared with Peirce and adequately worked out only in the context of Royce's mature semiotics, explains the moral predicament grounding his philosophy of loyalty. It also reflects the fundamental elements of his mature Christian theology. The immanent will to interpret is the Interpreter-Spirit; the Redeemer interprets the human condition (through teachings and atoning acts) and is a principal sign to be interpreted; and God is the whole infinite process in which interpretation is completed.

The Semiotic Account of Loyalty and Community

During the final year of his life, Royce commented in his metaphysics course: "If you answer the question as to what an individual human being is, you have answered all the questions in metaphysics." As we have seen, this is an old strategy for Royce. However, at this stage of his career, the strategy is expressed in terms of his theory of interpretation.

The first move is to note that an individual human being is a kind of group.

> The so-called individual man is in certain respects a social group. He consists of various selves. Anybody is more or less a multiple personality. This belongs to the normal plasticity and fecundity of social life.

The human being is a group of signs, each of which interprets the individual's past life and directs him towards the future. Each sign, insofar as it expresses his purposes, is a kind of self. Royce proceeds from here to note that the self (or each of the individual human's various selves) is not discovered introspectively, but must be expressed practically.

> The self isn't given, it is expressed in a life. You must be conscious of some enterprise, work, interest, concern. You are yourself by virtue of the fact that you are engaged in doing something. The coherence involves memory and expectation; you remember a past life and expect a future life... In consequence, every man has a life past and future as an essential part of him.[5]

The individual human being, then, is composed of many selves that are, in the optimal case, integrated into a single life. This account of the human individual is startlingly close to Royce's account of the community. Recall that Royce defines a community as a group of selves who interpret certain specific past events and certain expected future events as important parts of their lives. This seems to apply to the human individual. Royce notes:

> I don't see how you can define an individual as a life according to a plan, without saying that a community of interpretation, insofar as it is successful, is a self. The unity found in any one of the members is of the same nature as the unity of the larger entity. Any man is such a community of interpretation insofar as his present is interpreting his past to his future.[6]

All communities are selves and all selves are communities. Common memories and expectations are the ideals that integrate the thoughts of any individual and integrate the individual members of any larger community. They are signs. In the language of semiotics, community could be defined as an integrated process of interpretation, characterized by cooperative efforts of multiple selves to adequately interpret certain principal signs. For Royce, an adequate interpretation of some sign is the truth about that sign. Hence, all interpreters are (in one sense) truth seekers and all communities are communities of inquiry.

On this account, loyalty is the will to faithfully interpret community ideals. Consider, Royce asks, the case of some interpreter, B, who belongs to a community including other members A and C.

> So far as one's selfhood is the selfhood of the interpreter of a community, that is his main business, and to do it in one direction, that of addressing C on behalf of A. B is a self who desires to carry out a plan which furthers not A's will alone, or C's will alone, but to create and to make conscious and to carry out their united will, insofar as they are both to remain members of the community in which he remains an interpreter. Therefore B must be <u>loyal</u>, the willing and thoroughgoing servant of the cause and plan of C and A.[7]

In this abstract example, C and A could be thoughts of B, which B tries to integrate in a common plan. Or they could be other human beings who are each members of B's community. Or they could be large scale communities that work together in an even larger community. The permutations are endless. In each case, B's loyalty is the will to interpret the ideals of a community.

We see that moral life and loyalty progress through several stages. In the earliest stages – as in the life of infants and small children – the struggle is to coherently interpret one's own thought-signs. Without memory and other integrative cognitive processes (such as imitation and contrast), this struggle would never commence; the relations between thoughts would remain wholly sub-conscious.

This first stage of development, though social, inevitably produces a period of selfishness. Here the life plan consists of a variety of fragmentary efforts to gratify diverging impulses and desires. Maturity increases as the individual learns to harmonize her competing desires by recognizing higher desires and cultivating the self-control to subordinate lower desires (such as kicking one's brother) to these higher ones (such as avoiding TV restrictions).

Eventually selfishness becomes unfulfilling and the individual

home. These causes diverge considerably, but do not prevent the sisters from harmonious affiliation. In fact, it is quite possible that Amy's medical career will be enhanced by Phyllis' choice of a diverging cause. For instance, Phyllis may be able to help Amy understand how parents feel when they are forced to remain in the waiting room while their children are receiving sutures.

Even if causes diverge because they proceed from incompatible beliefs, it is possible to establish a degree of harmony. Japanese martial artists, for instance, tend to hold certain beliefs that flatly contradict dominant Western values. Nevertheless, it is quite possible for Western students to learn martial arts from Japanese teachers while retaining the distinctive and diverging elements of their own beliefs. Similarly, the beliefs of atheists and Christians are mutually inconsistent, but this does not prevent individuals of the two persuasions from establishing deep friendships or working together for certain common ideals. Many believe – and Royce would certainly be one of these – that a world including Japanese *Aikido* as well as American boxing, Christians and Hindus as well as atheists and humanists, is more interesting, richer and ultimately better than a world that lacks such variety. In the long run, major incompatibilities between these systems may be worked out, but to insist on establishing "the long run" in one fell swoop is a dangerous utopian fantasy.

Urgent problems with diverging loyalties occur, according to Royce, only when the divergence is of a forensic nature. This occurs when the ideals of one group state or imply that they must thwart or overturn the ideals of another group. For example, a commitment to human rights might require loyal Americans to intervene when powerless individuals in other countries are persecuted or murdered because of their ethnicity. War is a clear case of such forensic divergence. Royce does not think that we should promote pluralism of the sort that would inevitably cause forensic divergence of loyalties.

Second, Royce believes that divergence often promotes harmony by enhancing the rich complexity of human experience, thus providing opportunities for cooperative enterprise. This claim seems intuitively plausible. Phyllis and Amy provide one example. Martial arts styles that combine Oriental and Western techniques are another. Royce liked to illustrate this point with allusions to his favorite metaphor: music. Diverging loyalties, like the notes in a symphony, may be instructive. They may open the door to novelty and breadth of experience that would not be possible in a world of cultural uniformity or monotone noise. Through genuine loyalty, such novelty is transformed into a deeper understanding of reality.

> In unintelligently listening to music, one hears at first sounds; only later does one hear music... The musician's insight into music must involve... a true interpretation, a knowledge of that wherein the peculiar significance of the composition consisted.[10]

The peculiar significance of diverging loyalties is akin to this peculiar significance of notes in a musical composition. It is the extraordinary way in which very small things can be meaningful parts of something very big like a symphony or life itself. Various causes that are quite different on the surface may each be integral components of a vast, eternal process of self-discovery, undertaken by reality's ultimate composer.

Fallibilism Contra Relativism

As noted, the first thesis of fallibilism implies that any statement of fact can be false. Royce points out that for this thesis to make sense there must be a truth of the matter about things. That is, one cannot be a fallibilist if one denies the existence of truth. If there were no truth, then it would not be possible to err – our statements of fact would be neither right nor wrong; they would be meaningless.

This view may be of particular relevance today for two reasons. First, there are several prominent contemporary intellectuals who seem to deny the existence of truth – especially moral truth. Second, these denials, if Royce is right about the origin of fallibilism, contain the seeds of dogmatism and irrationalism. Let us see why.

In 1937, Charles L. Stevenson summarized the frustration of would-be moralists. When asking "Is X good?" Stevenson noted, "we are not concerned with "mere influence, mere advice." We are directing our inquiry into matters of truth. But this quest was, for Stevenson, deeply confusing.

> I can only answer that I do not understand. What is this truth to be about? ... I find no indefinable property, nor do I know what to look for.[11]

This confusion led Stevenson to conclude that moral terms were merely expressions of emotion. The statement "murder is immoral," for instance, was for Stevenson merely an expression of something like "I disapprove of murder." Stevenson claimed, in essence, that all specific moral judgments are grounded in emotion and hence that there is no transpersonal basis for truth in morality.

This idea became very popular in Stevenson's time and lingers in contemporary Western culture. Though the term "relativism" has many meanings, two varieties of ethical relativism can be traced to Stevenson's idea. The first I will call "crude ethical relativism" or CR. It can be stated as follows:

> CR: There is no truth of the matter about morality. Morality is purely a matter of personal feelings.

One rather obvious feature of CR is that it cannot be true. CR is a statement about morality. CR states that no statement about morality is true. Hence, if it is true, it cannot be true. If there is no truth of the matter about morality, then CR cannot be the truth of the matter about morality. In other words, CR is false.

For this reason, Stevenson and other philosophers generally have rejected CR. Some of these thinkers express ethical relativism as what I will call "ethical relativism about moral judgments" or RJ. RJ can be stated as follows:

> RJ: Moral judgments are not true or false, nor are they right or wrong. Our notions about what we ought to do are purely a matter of personal feelings. Further, our moral judgments cannot be justified by appeal to overarching moral theories or principles, because no such theory or principle is justified.

The term "moral judgments" in RJ means specific prescriptions for how we should act. RJ is not self-referentially inconsistent in the manner of CR, and so it may be a plausible hypothesis. RJ says that there is a truth of the matter about moral judgments. The truth is that these judgments do not possess the quality of being either true or false.

One major problem with RJ is that it implies that there are no moral obligations. Yet, oddly, some proponents of RJ interpret it to mean that we should be tolerant. Their argument goes something like this:

> Since every individual moral judgment is purely a matter of personal preference, then we should not pass judgment on other persons' moral judgments. We should respect the opinions of others and we should be tolerant of the cultural differences that underlie these opinions.

This argument, alas, is utter nonsense. If moral judgments are neither true nor false, neither right nor wrong, then a moral judgment that we ought to be tolerant cannot be right. Like any other moral judgment, it is merely a matter of personal feeling and carries no obligations. Intolerant cultures and intolerant individuals are just as valid as tolerant ones.

From a Roycean perspective, ethical relativism precludes an ethic of tolerance because it precludes the doctrine of fallibilism. If moral judgments cannot be wrong, then it makes no sense to say that they are fallible. The second and third theses of fallibilism – that we should be humble about our judgments and that we should support diverging strands of inquiry – amount to a prescription that we should be tolerant. But these theses have no basis if we rule out the first thesis, as ethical relativism does.

Dogmatism (in the sense of putting forth a view without reasons) is a predictable consequence of rejecting fallibilism. Ethical relativism tends to dogmatism because it denies the possibility of reasoning to moral conclusions and contains no basis for moral restraint. One who rejects any rational basis for morality is free to adopt whichever code of conduct he wants. Usually he will adopt a code that exalts his specific condition. The college professor who is a relativist will prescribe openness to new theories, since he is in the business of spinning out new theories, and will propagandize on behalf of the idea that only certain kinds of new theories – those like his – are worth talking about. Likewise, basketball-playing relativists will preach the virtues of athletics. And the serial murderer who is a relativist will challenge society – rhetorically – to refute him.

Of course, these tendencies are present in every individual. We all tend to see ourselves as the bright center of the universe. But, according to Royce, the search for truth is the means by which we overcome this inherent self-centeredness and join in the ethical fellowship that is both the meaning and the source of truth. Royce writes:

Human experience has, or can by the loyal efforts of truth seekers be made to possess, a real unity, superior in its nature and significance to the nature and significance of any detached observer's experience, more genuinely real than is the mere collection of the experiences of any set of detached observers, however large.[12]

The ethical relativist, by refusing to acknowledge the quest for moral truth, has created a shortcut to certainty. But Royce insists that inquiry should not be a quest for certainty. Certainty, Royce holds, is permanently elusive for the conscientious human inquirer. False certainty – as in the case of the relativist who confidently denounces the possibility of moral truth – is a barrier to community, since any community is, ultimately, a community of moral inquiry.

Scientific Inquiry

Like Peirce, Dewey and other pragmatists, Royce views science very broadly, and holds that physical and biological sciences are merely two species of a very generic form of inquiry (namely, interpretation). Because physical and biological scientists tend to be more sophisticated methodologists than many other inquirers, and because they have experienced some very notable and well-known successes, Royce thinks it is helpful to consult them in our efforts to understand the general nature of inquiry.

In this section we will examine the manner in which Royce's theory of interpretation applies in the physical and biological sciences. Three points will be highlighted: (1) the social nature of scientific inquiry, (2) the transcendental nature of the community of inquiry, and (3) the special office of "correlation."

Minot's Thesis

Let us begin with the theorist Laplace and let us imagine that Laplace is a family man whose children play with balloons. As he sips his morning coffee, Laplace is interrupted by a balloon that lands in his Cheerios. Wiping off the milk, he notices that the balloon is far from being a perfect sphere. The balloon has a small, flaccid protrusion. After much thought about this curious deformity, and the observation that it appears on other balloons as well, Laplace develops a hypothesis. It is a general law, he theorizes, that the wall tension of any hollow distensible object is directly related to the pressure within the object and to the radii of curvature of the object, according to the formula: $T = P/(1/Ra + 1/Rb)$. This phenomenon he calls, without excess humility, "the Law of Laplace." The protruding area on the balloon is flaccid because one of the radii of curvature is much smaller. This is intuitively plausible, and is consistent with the results of a few minor experiments Laplace is able to conduct in his laboratory.

"Now," Royce would ask, "Is the Law of Laplace confirmed? Is it an article of scientific knowledge?" "Not yet" is the reply. Before scientists are willing to accept this new hypothesis, they will have to test it for themselves. They will subject it to various angles of scrutiny. Biologists will ask if it works out in the case of hollow organs such as

90

veins and arteries. Aviation engineers will ask if it applies to fuel lines. In fact the Law of Laplace has worked out well in each of these scenarios. It explains, for instance, why arteries are thick-walled and veins are thin-walled (arteries have a much higher internal pressure) and why capillaries (which have very small radii) are thinnest of all.

The point of all this, for Royce, is that scientific inquiry is an inherently social enterprise. It begins with a presumably reproducible experience. When Laplace noted the conformity of his child's balloon, he assumed that, if present, other inquirers would observe this same conformity. If he were drunk, on the other hand, and saw a balloon playing the trumpet, he would probably conclude that he was having a hallucination – i.e., that other observers would not experience the same thing. In such cases, he would not try to formulate an hypothesis to explain how balloons can play the trumpet. On the other hand, he might try hypothesize about the causes of hallucinations.

The next step, after the occurrence of some unexplained, shared experience, is the formulation of an hypothesis. Even here the theorist is not entirely on his own. Generally he will consult others' theories and findings (as well as his own past experience). This brings us to where Laplace formulates his Law of Laplace. From here the social process continues – the hypothesis must be confirmed by others. Royce notes that the necessity of confirmation by peers is well recognized amongst scientists, and summarized in what he calls Minot's theses (after an eminent Harvard scientist):

> In that lecture "On the Method of Science" Professor Minot carefully expounded, and very extensively illustrated, the thesis that, while natural science is dependent upon the experiences of individuals for every one of its advances in the knowledge of the facts of nature, no experience of any individual man can count as a scientific discovery until it has been sufficiently confirmed by other and independent observers.[13]

In scientific inquiry, the theorist is only one contributor in a series of triadic interpretations. The first triad consists of (1) an experience attributed to all or potentially all human observers as principal, (2) the theorist as interpreter, and (3) the theorist's hypothesis as interpretant. A succeeding triad involves (1) the theorist's hypothesis as principal, (2) the colleague or critic to whom the hypothesis is presented as interpreter, and (3) a basic appraisal of the meaning and significance of the hypothesis as the interpretant. Finally, there is a triad that includes (1) an appraisal of the meaning of the hypothesis in terms of an experiment designed to test its consequences, (2) a scientist who conducts the experiment, and (3) the results of this experiment. Of course, several experiments will require interpretation, then perhaps more testing. Royce summarizes this process in terms of a larger triadic structure:

> The scientific community consists, at the least, of the original discoverer, of his interpreter, and of the critical worker who tests or controls the discoverer's observations by means of new experiences devised for that purpose.[14]

This triadic, communal structure is necessary in applied science as well as in physics, chemistry or biology. Medicine, for instance, begins with the experience of being ill. A malady like high blood pressure would not be a problem to investigate, would not be a disease, would not even be measured or considered "high," unless it led to unpleasant experiences for human beings. Medicine's original theorist, then, must be someone who is interpreting the experience of another. Further, no theory of medicinal effects is confirmed until it helps patients. Illness is primarily experienced as a disruption in the life plan of the individual who is ill. The amelioration or cure of illness occurs when this disruption is alleviated or eliminated. Scientific inquiry in the health sciences, then, begins and ends in the experience of laypersons. If people had no loyalties, no plans, no desires, then illness would not occur (since one physical state would be no better or worse than any other).

The Transcendental Nature of the Community of Inquiry

A second feature of scientific inquiry, according to Royce, is its implicit and necessary faith in the existence of a community of interpreters. Royce writes:

> This appeal to the scientific community implies a belief that there is such a community... This belief in the reality of the scientific community is itself no belief in a fact which is open to the scientific observations of any individual. No observer of nature has ever discovered, by the methods used in his or in any natural science, that there exists any such community. The existence of the community of scientific observers is known through interpretation. This interpretation expresses essentially social motives, as well as profoundly ethical motives. And this interpretation is also of a type which we are obliged to use in

dealing with the whole universe.[15]

Royce is claiming here that belief in the existence of a community of interpretation is a necessary condition for scientific inquiry. We can't even do science if we don't implicitly hold this belief. Royce adds, that the existence of such a community is, in fact, a transcendental condition for the scientific progress we have experienced.

Recall from the first chapter that a transcendental condition for some X is a condition that must pertain in order for X to occur. That is, X could not be a feature of human experience unless the transcendental conditions of X are met. For Kant, who lacked Royce's notion of the Absolute, transcendental conditions were necessarily categories of the perceiving or conceiving intellect. They were cognitive structures that we bring to experience. For Royce, however, transcendental conditions are characteristics of reality, which is communal. They are not merely cognitive, since they presuppose the purposeful (voluntaristic) function provided by the will to interpret.

If Royce is correct, then scientific inquiry provides another transcendental argument for the existence of the Absolute. Further, and perhaps more importantly from a practical point of view, the community of scientific inquirers is of necessity a branch of the great community of all humanity. Science expresses and fulfills humanity's deepest purposes. And loyal pursuit of scientific truth, when sincere, is an expression of loyalty to the great community. The standard for scientific investigation is genuine loyalty.

> When the sciences teach us to get rid of superstition, they do this by virtue of a loyalty to the pursuit of truth which is, as a fact, loyalty to the cause of the spiritual unity of mankind: an unity which the students of science conceive in terms of an unity of our human experience of nature, but which, after all, they more or less unconsciously interpret just as all the other loyal souls interpret their causes; namely, as a genuine living reality, a life superior in type to the individual lives which we lead – worthy of devoted service, significant, and not merely an incidental play of a natural mechanism.[16]

Correlation and Correlators

One important form of scientific interpretation is what Royce calls "correlation."[17] Correlation is the office of one who explains scientific theories to people who need to appropriate these theories. In our example of the Law of Laplace, this process might involve an explanation of the implications of the Law for medicine, for engineering, or for communication technology.

Correlation, in a wider sense, is the interpretation of any form of specialized information to a needful public. Correlation is exceedingly important in societies that depend on rapid and accurate dissemination of knowledge. Within the current "information revolution," we are experiencing a remarkable proliferation of persons who make a living as correlators. Their ranks include journalists, Web site coordinators, professional liaisons, congressional aids, lobbyists, experts who appear in the media or in court, and many others. For Royce, one typical correlator, present in any epoch, is the philosopher.

Though it is true – even necessary – that scientific investigators and most others will for the most part view their cause in relatively narrow terms, it is incumbent on the philosopher to understand and to articulate connections between these various activities and the causes they express.

> Philosophers have actually devoted themselves, in the main, neither to perceiving the world, nor to spinning webs of conceptual theory, but to interpreting the meaning of the civilizations which they have represented, and to attempting the interpretation of whatever minds in the universe, human or divine, they believe to be real. That the philosophers are neither the only interpreters, nor the chiefs among those who interpret, we now well know. The artists, the leaders of men, and all the students of the humanities, make interpretation their business; and the triadic cognitive function, as the last lecture showed, has its applications in all the realms of knowledge. But in any case the philosopher's ideals are those of an interpreter. He addresses one mind and interprets another. The unity which he seeks is that which is characteristic of a community of interpretation.[18]

In the age of applied philosophy – where bioethicists, business ethicists, environmental ethicists and other such practical thinkers abound – Royce's version of philosophy seems perfectly at home. For Royce, philosophy is a response to real problems. Towards pain and illness, poverty and strife, emptiness and desperation, the Roycean philosopher directs an empathic gaze. But one eye is always aimed at the horizon. For Royce, the eternal and the practical are melded organically. In the long run, we cannot address one without addressing the other. Indeed, "the real world is simply the true interpretation of this our problematic situation."

94

Endnotes

1. Charles Sanders Peirce, *The Essential Peirce: Selected Philosophical Writings*, Vol. 1, ed. Nathan Houser and Christian Kloesel (Bloomington and Indianapolis: Indiana University Press, 1992), 149.

2. Parts of this section are adapted from two earlier works: Griffin Trotter, "Royce, Community and Ethnicity," *Transactions of the Charles S. Peirce Society* 30 (Spring, 1994): 231-269; and Griffin Trotter, *The Loyal Physician: Roycean Ethics and the Practice of Medicine* (Nashville: Vanderbilt University Press, 1997), 85-95.

3. Peirce held that there is a rudimentary manner in which the chair (unconsciously) interprets its prior states to its future states. Physical objects, he claimed, take habits. The laws of physics and biology are deeply engrained habits.

4. Quotation from Peirce's unpublished manuscripts, cited in Vincent Colapietro, *Peirce's Approach to the Self: A Semiotic Perspective on Human Subjectivity* (Albany, New York: State University of New York Press, 1989), 114.

5. This and the proceeding quotation are from Josiah Royce, *Metaphysics: His Philosophy 9 Course of 1915-1916 as stenographically recorded by Ralph W. Brown and complemented by notes from Byron F. Underwood*, Initial Editor William Ernest Hocking, Co-edited by Richard Hocking and Frank Oppenheim (Albany, New York: Sate University of New York Press, 1998), 19. Hereafter this work will be abbreviated RMC.

6. RMC, 26

7. RMC, 25.

8. Epistemology is the study of knowledge. To say that everything is epistemically vulnerable is to say that knowledge is never established beyond all possible refutation.

9. RMC, 50.

10. RMC, 88.

11. Charles L. Stevenson, "The Emotive Meaning of Ethical Terms," *Mind* 46 (1937): 30.

12. WJ, 85.

13. PC, 322.

14. PC, 331.

15. PC, 324.

16. WJ, 92.